MARJORIE PHILLIPS AND HER PAINTINGS

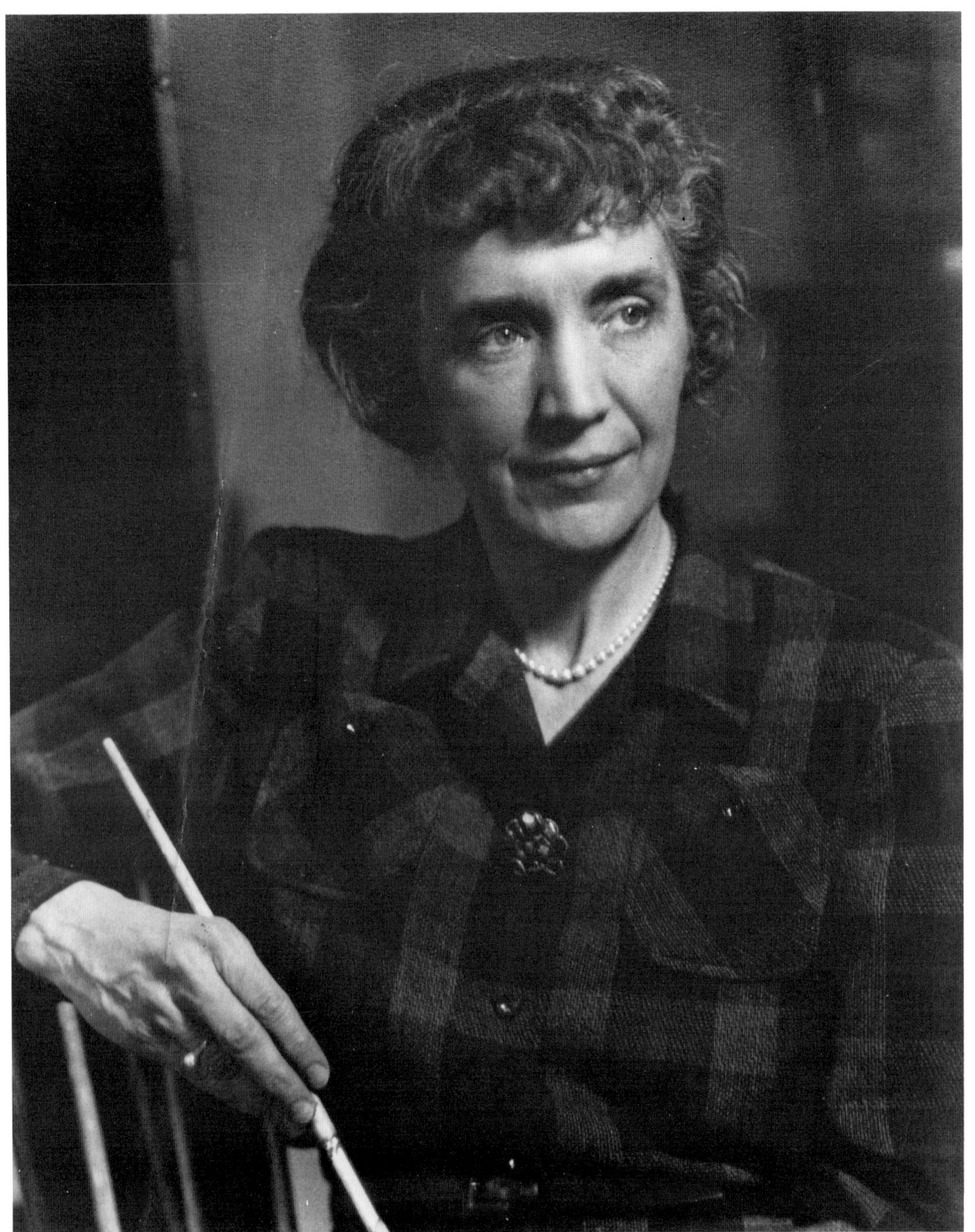

PHOTO BY F. VOGEL 1940

Marjorie Phillips and her Paintings

By MARJORIE PHILLIPS

Edited by Sylvia Partridge

W. W. NORTON & COMPANY
New York · London

Published simultaneously in Canada by Penguin Books Canada Ltd,
2801 *John Street, Markham, Ontario* L3R 1B4
Printed in the United States of America
First Edition
ISBN 0-393-02290-0

ACKNOWLEDGMENTS

My greatest thanks go to Sylvia Partridge, who first thought of my doing this book and who has managed the project with sustained interest and constant enthusiasm.

During all stages Laughlin Phillips has been of extraordinary help with frequent consultations, and especially in his suggestions of outstanding people in the fields of photography and printing. Liza Phillips has also contributed suggestions and has helped with the proofreading.

Barbara Gasper has provided true and unflagging interest and support.

Pep II, my schnauzer, has kept us in extra good humor during the work.

Most of the color transparencies were made by Bob Grove, and the book was designed and the printing of the reproductions was supervised by Bert Clarke.

And thanks also for all the generous help from the staff of The Phillips Collection.

CONTENTS

Foreword *by Laughlin Phillips* ix

Reminiscences 3

Color plates and comments 25

Notes and drawings 101

Exhibition history 121

Index 123

FOREWORD

My mother, Marjorie Phillips, died June 19, 1985, after an extraordinarily rich and creative life. For over seventy years she had managed to set aside part of every possible day to work as an artist. In these informal memoirs, written in the months surrounding her ninetieth birthday, she tells what art and her own painting meant to her, how she came to paint certain pictures, and how she felt about other artists and esthetic doctrines. It is the story of an independent, dedicated, and disciplined artist, gentle in spirit, but strong of will.

Willpower was definitely needed to find time each day to work in the studio, because as the wife of an impulsive, energetic collector, writer, and museum founder, my mother found herself ever more called upon to play the roles of advisor, companion, organizer, hostess, mother, and museum executive. And when Duncan Phillips died in 1966, she succeeded him for six years as director of The Phillips Collection—a period in which she organized a major international exhibition of Paul Cézanne and wrote the book, *Duncan Phillips and His Collection.*

I have strong childhood memories of her studios in Washington and Pennsylvania, redolent of turpentine and fixative, full of tacks and charcoal and rolls of canvas. Except when impressed into service as a restless model, I was not often to be found in the studios (or particularly welcome there). They functioned as workshop sanctuaries in which my mother, I feel quite sure, found her most solid and satisfying sense of identity.

As these memoirs reveal, her painting always reflected a conscious decision, made early in life, to paint the sort of pictures which give pleasure, celebrate the beauties of life, and reveal the vital essence of her subjects. From her poetic, impressionistic early work to the more assertive and striking later paintings, there is always a disarmingly direct, sensitive, and appreciative vision.

I am most grateful to my cousin, Sylvia Partridge, who first conceived the idea of this book and persuaded my mother to launch it through a series of recorded interviews. Typically, however, my mother later decided to assume the more arduous task of writing the book herself, in longhand. Sylvia has very ably organized the project, serving as researcher and editor, working with photographers, printers, and sometimes reluctant lenders. It is a book which gives me great pleasure, since I was sometimes too young, or too close, or too absorbed in self to seek out the meaning of what was happening in those studios. It sustains my feeling that the work of a very talented and dedicated artist may sometimes have been cramped and obscured by the growth and demands of the Collection itself. In any case, as this book will attest, my mother at ninety, though no longer able to paint every day in her studio, was still thinking as an artist.

Laughlin Phillips

To celebrate
the wonder of the world
with color and form
in art

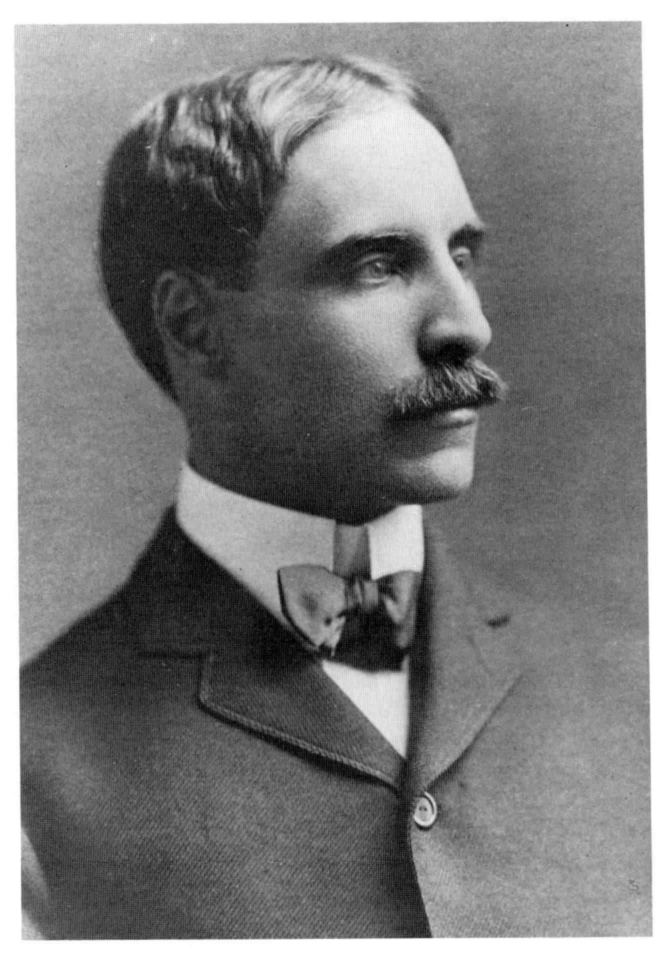

My father, Charles Ernest Acker (1868–1920)

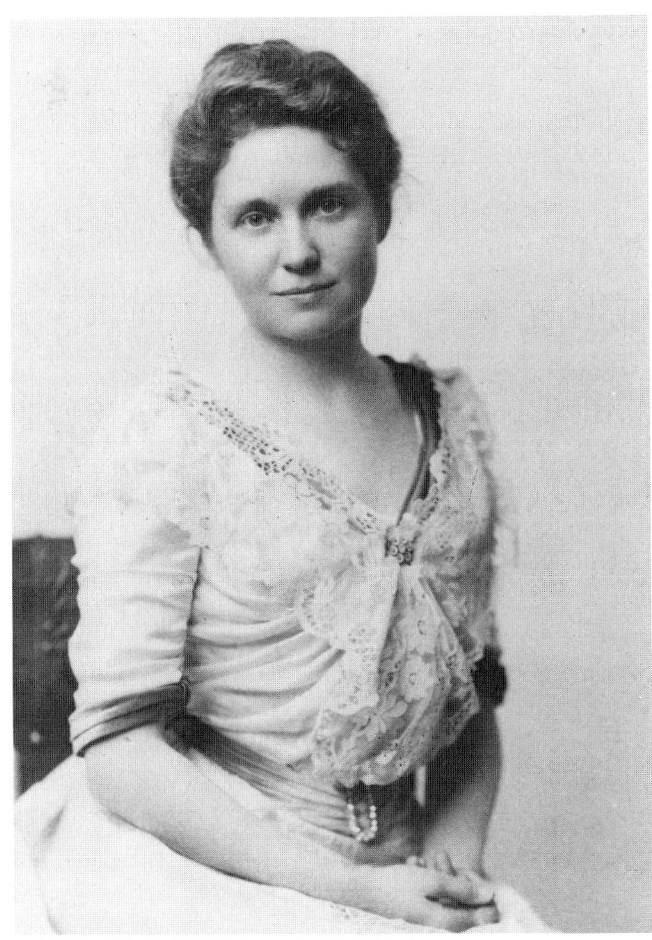

My mother, Alice Beal Acker (1868–1952)

REMINISCENCES

I was born in Bourbon, Indiana, on October 25, 1894, when my parents were on the way from Chicago to East Orange, New Jersey. Father had left his job with Western Electric in Chicago and the family had stopped in Bourbon to visit my father's parents, William James and Mercia Grant Acker. I was born ahead of schedule. Mother wanted to name me after Father's mother, Mercia Grant, but she didn't like the name Mercia so she settled for Marjorie instead. I'm glad she did because I like the name Marjorie. My middle name was Grant, after Ulysses S. Grant, a second cousin of Grandmother Acker.

My father, Charles Ernest Acker, was an inventor and manufacturer. He was distinguished looking, very handsome, and had high standards for us, making sure we knew good people. He cared very much. He was a little bit distant, but on the other hand when we were quite young he used to read to us a lot—Kipling and all sorts of good books. He had a fine library of his own and played the piano.

My mother, Alice Beal Acker, was one of the six children of William Reynolds and

Eleanor Louise Beal, my maternal grandparents' family that played such a significant role in my life. She was a lively person with a good sense of humor, and appreciated art. She and Father had six children: Eleanor, myself, Ernest, Alice, William and Mary Elizabeth.

We stayed in Bourbon, Indiana for only two months before going on to East Orange, New Jersey, where Father worked on various chemical experiments. Some time later the family moved to Niagara Falls, New York, where Father started his own company and built a plant. We lived there for about six or seven years.

Mother took us to visit Buffalo, New York, several times while we were living in Niagara Falls. In 1901 we went to the Pan American Exposition. I remember the Japanese tea houses. It was a fascinating and well done exposition, and had great charm. In 1905 we went to the Albright Art Gallery, one of the first important museums in the country. The Albright Art Gallery had a very rich collection of old masters as well as pictures that were contemporary then. It was overwhelming to be in a museum dedicated with such intensity to art. The building was attractive and stately, pure Grecian in style.

In 1907 Father suffered a severe business setback. It was a great tragedy as he lost everything. Mother was heartbroken and never fully recovered her health. Shortly afterwards, we left Niagara Falls and moved to New York City where we lived for two years at the city home of our maternal grandparents at 1 West 121st Street. It was a lovely neighborhood at that time, just on the edge of Mt. Morris Park.

My older sister, Eleanor, and I started drawing when we were about five. We used to draw big houses with all the rooms and partitions. From the age of eleven on, I painted every day. I painted the things around me, the landscape, the people, in oil and watercolor. I painted from the sheer need to paint. Art has always been of vital importance to me.

My sisters and brothers and I spent part of each summer at "Wilellyn," the estate of my maternal grandparents in Newburgh, New York. "Wilellyn" was a name that

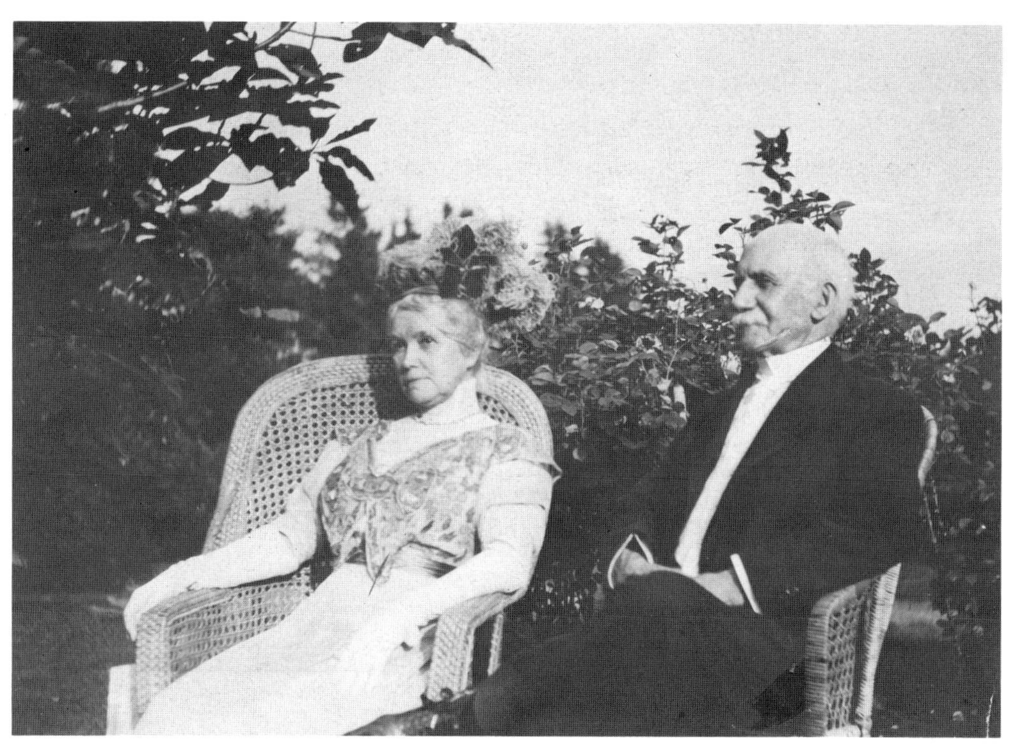

My maternal grandparents, Eleanor Louise Beal (1840–1921) *and William R. Beal* (1838–1912)

combined the names of my grandparents, William and Eleanor Beal, and was a very special and wonderful place to go. All the grandchildren had a passion for it. The house was perched on a steep hill overlooking the Hudson River. At the foot of the hill was a vegetable garden with a grape arbor around it. Two of my uncles were artists, Gifford and Reynolds Beal, and they had a large studio on the top floor. Oh, the tubes of paint and the palettes. The canvases. The dedication to art . . . the feeling of the importance of art! I must have had the same feeling in me, to respond so strongly. I must have been born with it in me, and it was pretty much throughout the Beal family. Certainly my mother encouraged me in my artistic interests, although Father was against the idea of my becoming an artist, at first, because I was a girl. He tried to discourage me from going to art school.

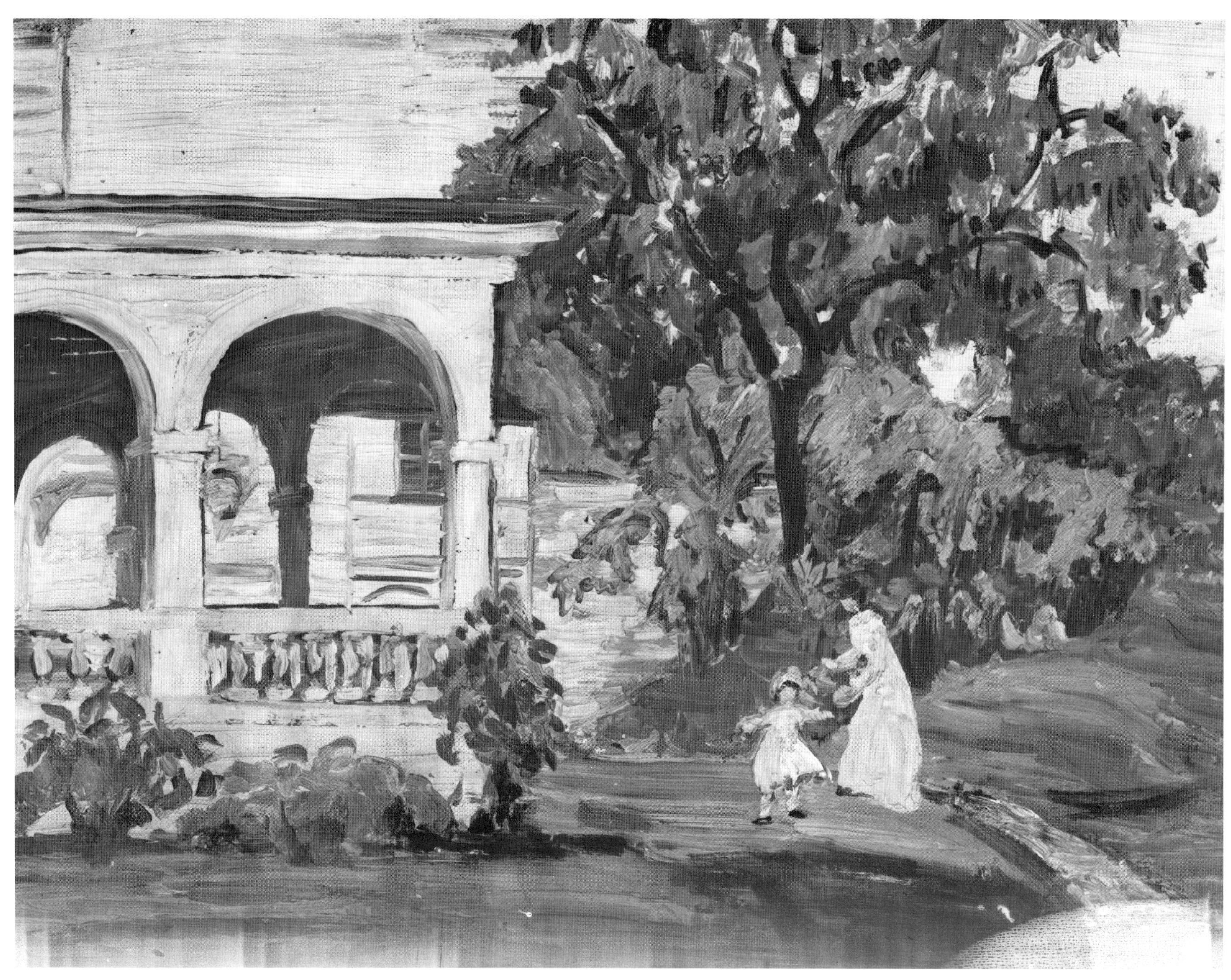

Corner of the house at Ossining, facing the Hudson River. c. 1914 *(Marjorie Acker).*
Oil on wood panel, 12⅜ × 15¼ *inches. Estate of the Artist.*

It was through the encouragement of my uncles that I made the decision to become an artist. That must have been around 1911, when I was sixteen. I think I would have done it anyway, but it was seeing their work and spending time in their studio that was particularly inspiring. They didn't try to influence me.

In 1909 we moved into a lovely romantic house located on a bluff above the Hudson River at Ossining, New York, with a sweeping view of the river. Here father started a nitrogen company. I lived there until my marriage in 1921. Unfortunately, father died in 1920 after a protracted illness, just a year before my marriage.

My life was happy in Ossining. I was exceedingly fond of the place. There was an old fashioned lilac bush right outside my bedroom window. I would wake up in the morning and see it. And I did a lot of things with the children. I always loved children, and used to give parties for them. There were little tea parties and maypole parties. We had a great deal of fun. I had a very happy childhood. I think I was lucky.

The painting illustrated on the opposite page shows a corner of our house at Ossining. The figures on the lawn are my mother and my youngest sister, Mary Elizabeth.

A great friend of the family during our stay in New York City was Miss Virginia Gerson, a very lovable and wonderful person. She was the sister-in-law of William Merritt Chase, a prominent and distinguished artist and teacher who influenced many artists of his time, and it was she who suggested that we start "The Magazine." She said William Merritt Chase's children had a magazine and she suggested that we children would enjoy doing that. So we did start a magazine after moving to Ossining. I was editor-in-chief and got the material together. There were poems, drawings, stories and jokes—all contributed by family members and friends. The magazine lasted for two or three years.

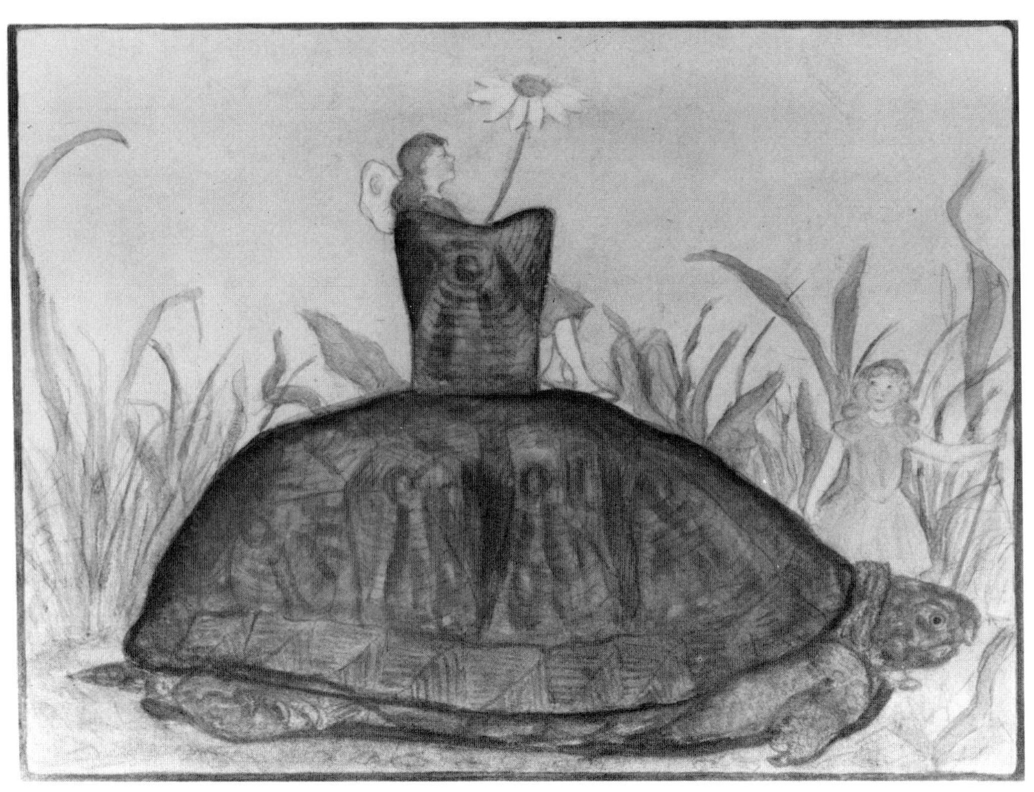

1911 *(Marjorie Acker). Watercolor on paper,* 6⅞ × 9⅛ *inches. Mrs. John Lyman, San Rafael, California.*

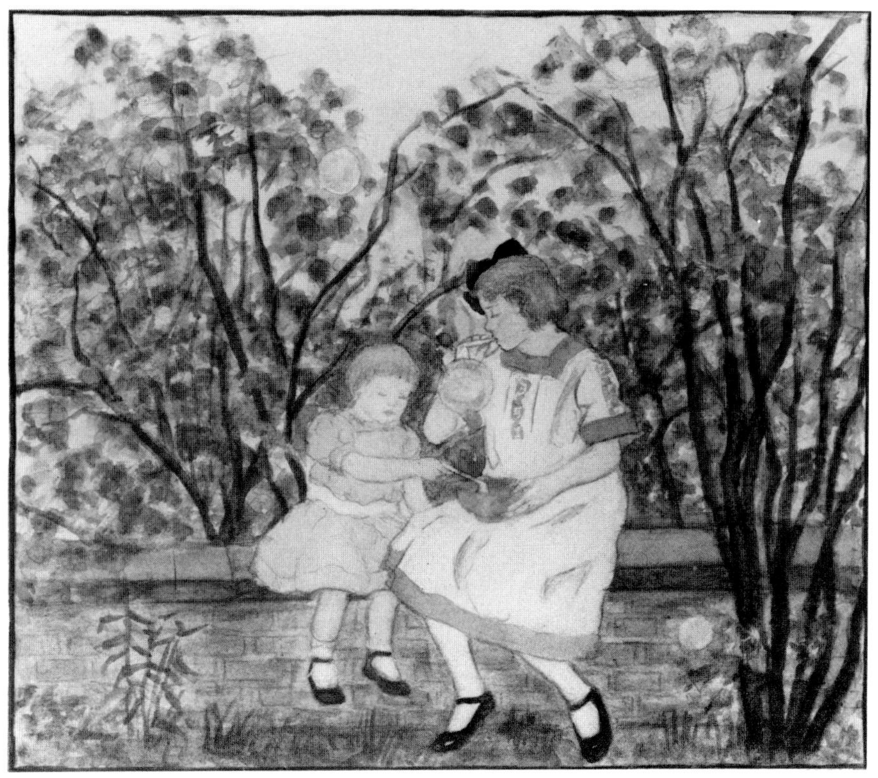

1910 *(Marjorie Acker). Watercolor on paper,* 7⅛ × 8 *inches. Mrs. John Lyman, San Rafael, California.*

Three of the illustrations that I contributed to "The Magazine" are included here. The first one is of a fairy who holds a sunflower and is riding in the howdah on top of a turtle. I saw many turtles when I was growing up because my youngest brother, William, kept them in a pen right outside my window in Ossining. Here the fairy is going for a ride, a pleasure trip, accompanied by another fairy. Something like going for a ride in Central Park, New York City, in a horse and carriage. My sister Eleanor and I imagined that we had quite a few fairies in our garden. The idea of fairies is so poetic.

The two children blowing bubbles in the second illustration are my sister Alice and my younger brother William. Soap bubbles are still with us. I think they always will be because they're so magical.

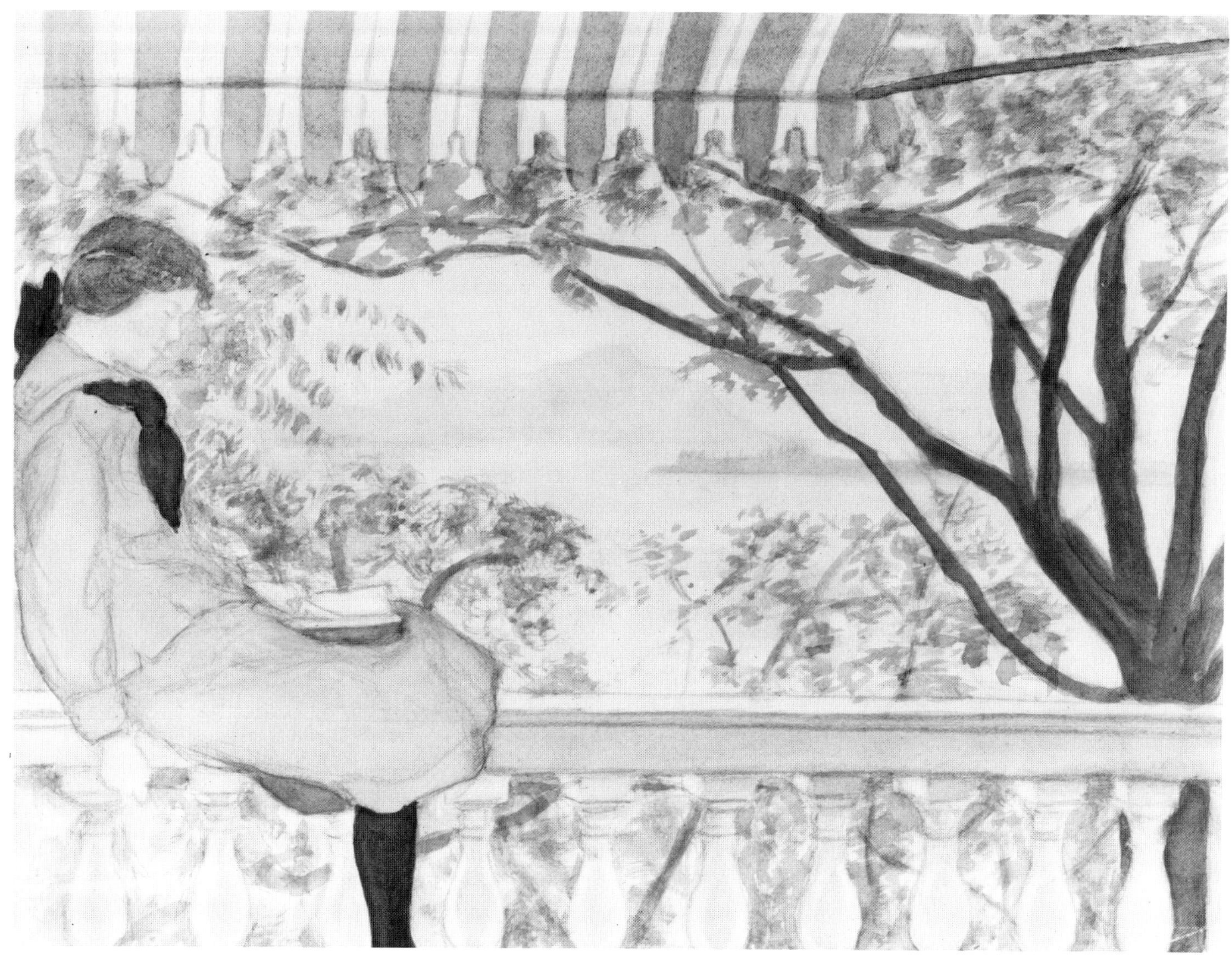

c. 1912 *(Marjorie Acker).*
Watercolor on paper,
8⅜ × 11 *inches.*
Estate of the Artist.

The third illustration of a girl sitting on a balustrade overlooking the Hudson River looks quite a bit like me. It gives an idea of how Eleanor and I dressed in those days. Black stockings and a tie. In the distance is Croton Point and, across the river, Bear Mountain. Two of my favorite books that I could have been reading in this painting were *Castle Blair,* a book that seems to have been forgotten, and *Black Beauty.*

Mother and father had lovely friends in Ossining, and they gave dinners frequently. There was always a lot going on—it was a lively life.

On the opposite page is an early painting of a family dinner, painted about 1912. My mother and father are seated at the heads of the table. The other seated figures are uncles and aunts, various friends, and children. The girl seated next to my mother is my youngest sister, Mary Elizabeth, to whom the painting now belongs. This was probably Thanksgiving because of the tray of fruit in the middle of the table. The topmost fruit on the tray is a pineapple, the symbol of hospitality. I feel that the bowl on the mantel is good, it's just right, a sharp focus.

I went to Miss Fuller's School for Girls in Ossining. Miss Fuller was a very past-generation person. She would read some beautiful, inspiring thing every morning—not a prayer, but something inspiring. She would start the day for the girls that way. I was always very interested. The school was full of good teachers. I particularly liked the English classes and always received high marks, and our ancient history teacher brought her subject alive—it so fascinated her students. I loved basketball. Being tall, I could toss the ball very well and get it in, you know.

There was an art teacher at Miss Fuller's School but my uncles advised me not to study with her as they felt she probably wasn't a first rate artist, and I took their advice.

The last doll that was given to me was when I was 15—a baby doll with a long skirt, the old-fashioned type. I loved dolls. I remember when Father wanted to give away our wonderful stockinette dolls to our cousins who had less than we had. We children were just heartbroken and couldn't imagine he didn't know that to us they were real people.

It was about 1917 or 1918 that I went to the Art Students League in New York City, an art school that had the reputation of being the best of its day. Eleanor and I took turns

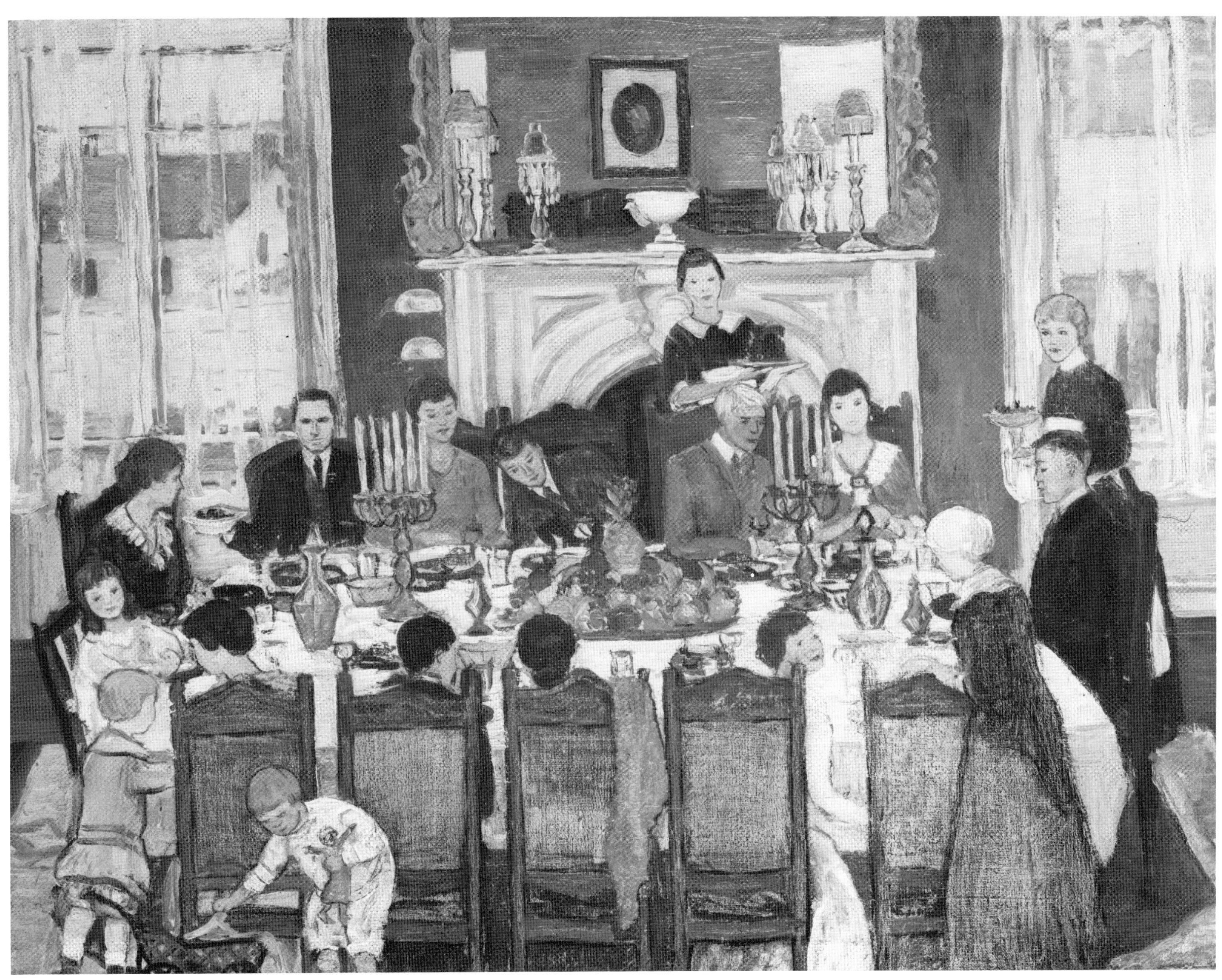

'Family at Dinner.' c. 1916 *(Marjorie Acker). Oil on canvas,* 16×20 *inches. Mrs. John Lyman, San Rafael, California.*

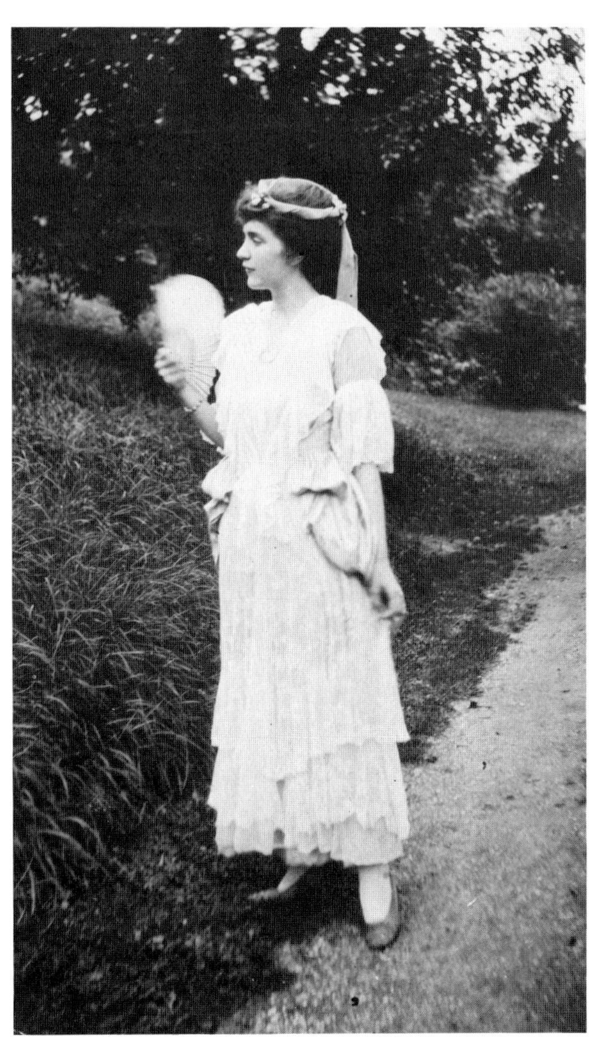

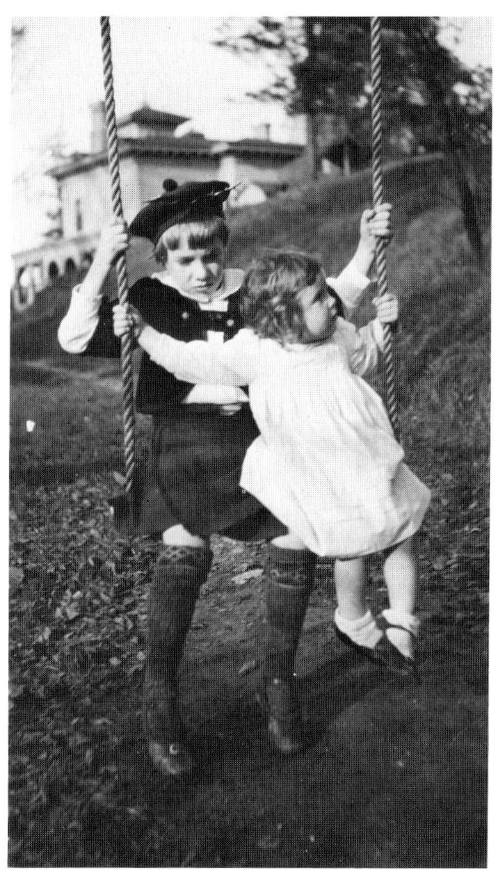

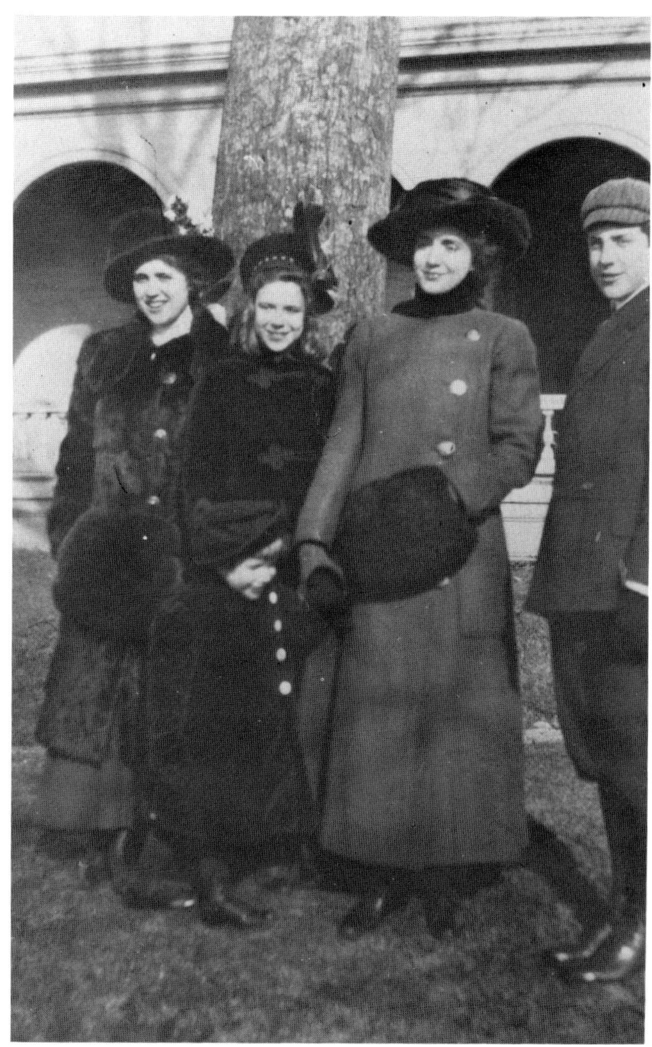

Above, from left to right: my sisters and brothers, William, Mary Elizabeth, Eleanor, Alice, myself, and Ernest.

Left: myself in costume for a French play at Miss Fuller's School.

going. I would go one year, and she would go the next because Mother wasn't well. When I was at home, I would play with the younger children. I also painted at home, and tried to have a schedule. Discipline has been an important part of my painting career.

To get to school, I would take the train along the Hudson River from Ossining to Grand Central Station on 42nd Street in New York City. Then I would walk to the Art Students League on 57th Street, past the many art galleries that were spread out along Fifth Avenue at that time. There were so many things displayed in the windows, and I'd go to all the exhibitions on my way. Sometimes I'd go to the Metropolitan Museum, which was just as exciting as art school. I loved the stimulation of New York.

I had a composition class with Boardman Robinson, who was outstanding. He talked about design, rhythmic continuity, pattern. "Rhythmic continuity" was a phrase which spoke to me. It means caught up and working together, not just scattered. It has to do with overall pattern, direction, eye travel. That's what Boardman Robinson stressed. He had a gift for putting his ideas into words. He was encouraging.

Another of my teachers was Kenneth Hayes Miller. I took an oil painting class from him, and only saw him for about five minutes once a week. Sometimes he'd say, "That's good." He was encouraging in a general sort of way, and left me pretty much to myself.

I was a rather lone figure at the art school, especially since I was a day student and commuting to my home in Ossining. One of my few friends was named Harriet. We used to go to the Société Anonyme, which was the most modern gallery in New York at that time. It was just two or three rooms in a house, and had been started by Katherine Dreier (who later included one of my paintings in her collection).

Gifford Beal was president of the Art Students League during that period, and I used to see him from time to time. He had a studio apartment on 59th Street, and had asked me to bring in my paintings whenever I wanted. He and his wife, Maude, were just dear to all their nieces and nephews. Often I would take my work over to his apartment in the afternoon for discussion, and then take the afternoon train home. One day in January, 1921, Uncle Giff sent me a card, an invitation to the Phillips Memorial Gallery Exhibition at the Century Club, to which he belonged. Of course, I went. It was there that I met Duncan Phillips, the founder of the Phillips Memorial Gallery, who had come up from his home in Washington, D.C., to be present at the opening.

When I first met Duncan Phillips, I knew. I knew that art had the same tremendous meaning for both of us and that we would probably marry. I think Duncan knew too because he immediately began sending me books and flowers and all sorts of things, and several months later we were engaged.

I remember one day during our engagement, Duncan and I were walking along a grass path near my home in Ossining that led down to Father's laboratory, an old converted casino. There was a swing on one of the big trees part way down. Duncan sat down in the swing. My brothers and sisters and I pushed him, and he swung higher and higher. Duncan laughed, and we all laughed and enjoyed ourselves. He had a youthful spirit.

During our engagement, Duncan used to send me Marshall Neil roses. I loved them, and at the time that I should have been getting ready for the wedding I decided to paint them. In fact I felt impelled to paint them. The painting is illustrated on the opposite page and was done rather heavily with a palette knife. A big bowl of roses. I eventually gave the painting to Mother Phillips even though she probably did not appreciate that style of painting, but I was under a strong impulsion.

Duncan and I were married at my parents' home in Ossining on October 8, 1921. After our honeymoon, we moved into Duncan's family home in Washington, D.C., with Mother Phillips and lived with her until her death in 1929. The house is on the corner of

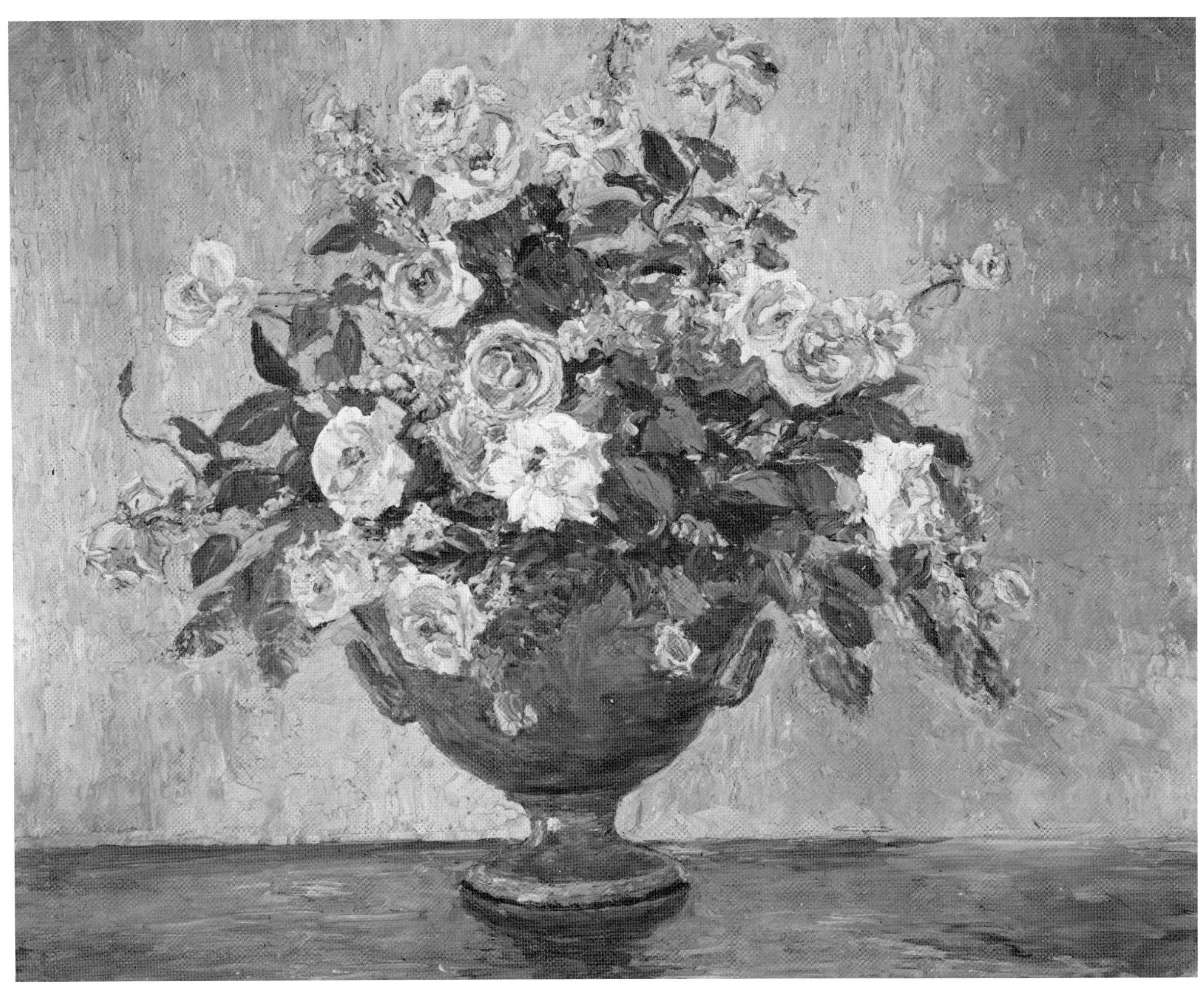

'Marshall Neil Roses.' 1921 *(Marjorie Acker). Oil on canvas,* 29¼ × 35¾ *inches. Estate of the Artist.*

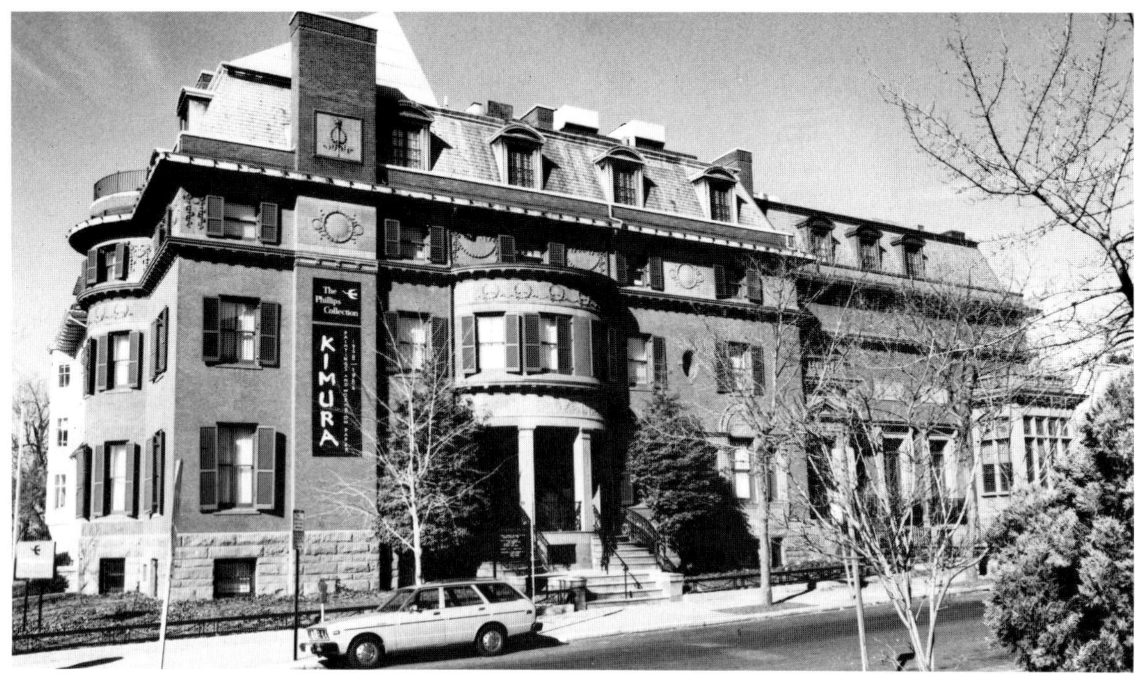

A current photograph of the Phillips family home, now The Phillips Collection.
PHOTO BY SYLVIA PARTRIDGE

21st and Q Streets and Massachusetts Avenue, and is now given over completely to The Phillips Collection.* We had two children: Mary Marjorie and Laughlin.

Women were beginning to go into art during those years. Mother Phillips used to say "Marjorie sketches." That sounded better to her than "Marjorie is a painter." That was the attitude of the older generation, but the younger ones were beginning to try their wings. I sometimes used to feel a little guilty about painting, but I was an artist when I married and I trusted myself. Of course Duncan knew that I was a painter and knew that I would continue to paint. He encouraged me to continue.

One of the paintings that I did during the first year after our marriage was *The North Library*, shown on the opposite page. I loved the spaciousness of that room with the tall windows and the great bay windows at one end and, at the other end, the Steinway grand

* The name of the museum has changed over the years as follows: 1920–1921 Phillips Memorial Art Gallery; 1921–1948 Phillips Memorial Gallery; 1948–1961 The Phillips Gallery; 1961–present The Phillips Collection.

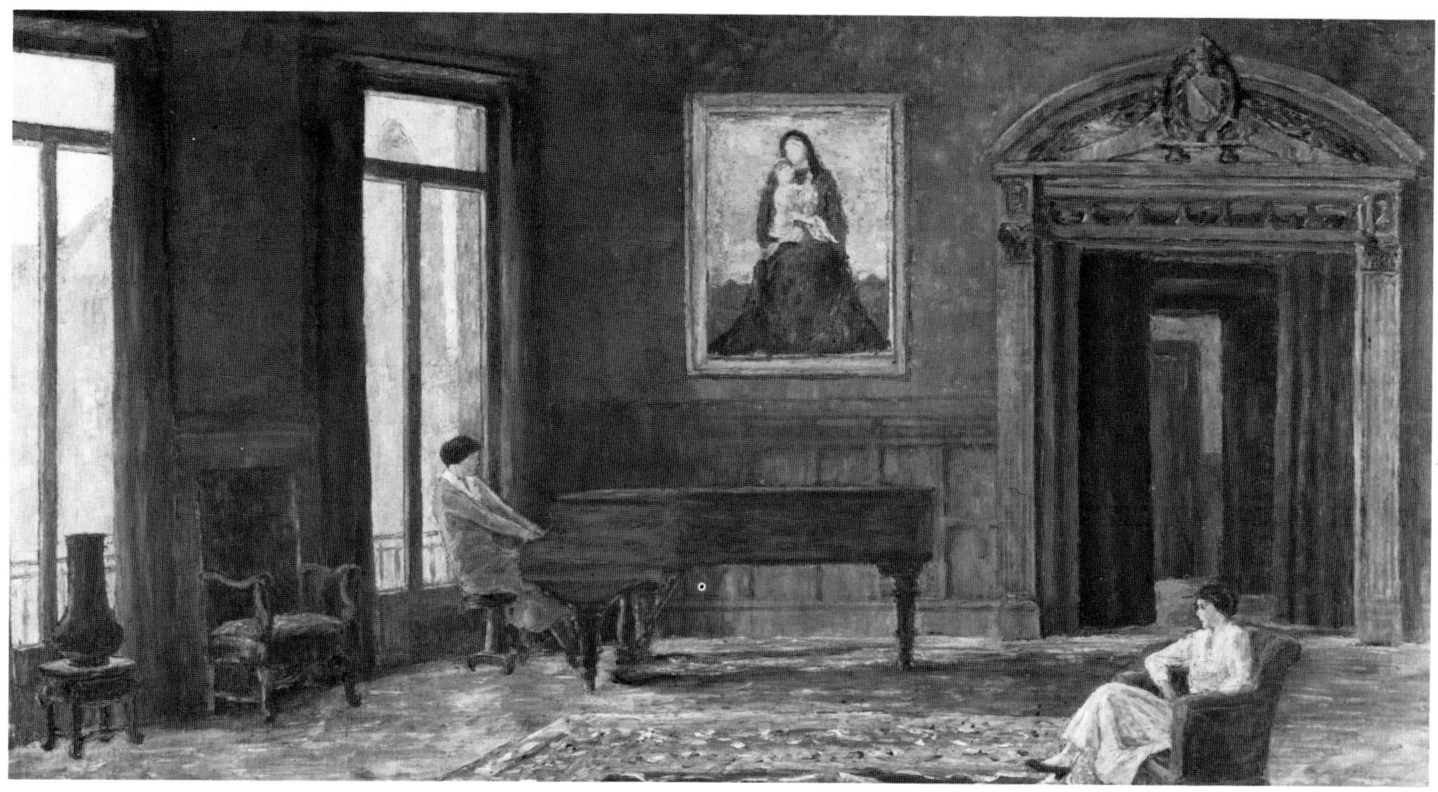

'The North Library.' 1922. *Oil on canvas,* 17 × 32 *inches. The Phillips Collection.*

piano. The figure at the piano might be my sister Alice and the seated figure, listening, could be myself. The painting of the madonna and child is by Augustus Vincent Tack. The big vase looks as if it might be for long stem American Beauty roses, it's so tall.

There was a billiard table at the other end of the room. Both Duncan and his father, Major Duncan Clinch Phillips, loved to play billiards and were good at it. There were quite a few books that lined the room on each side a little more than half way up, all behind glass. The room was also used for large dinner parties that were given about four times a year until Mother Phillips' last illness. The dining table ran the length of the room, and there were usually about forty people. The everyday dining room was next door, and the kitchen was in the basement. The food was sent up by dumbwaiters to the pantry.

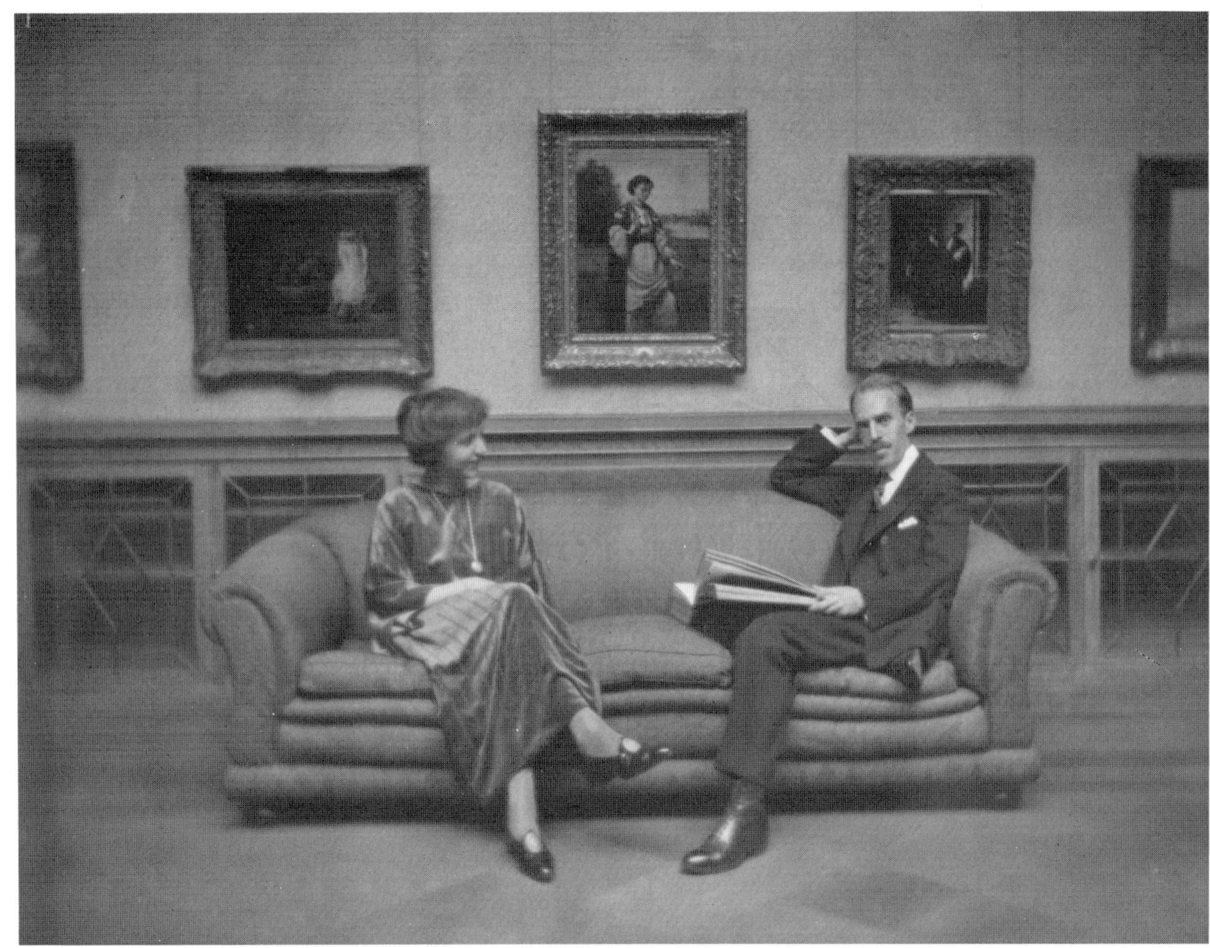

Duncan and I in the north library, shortly after our marriage.
PHOTO BY CLARA SIPRELL

As Duncan's wife I had a lot of executive and social responsibilities. I used to sometimes say to myself that I was like a prestidigitator—you know, someone who does tricks, throwing oranges, and so on. My days were spent juggling different roles: painting in the mornings; running the house; being a mother; fulfilling social responsibilities, which we kept at a minimum; and, after Duncan's death in 1966, running the gallery until Laughlin took over in 1972. I didn't mind it because I had so many satisfactions. I was happy as long as I had some time to paint every day.

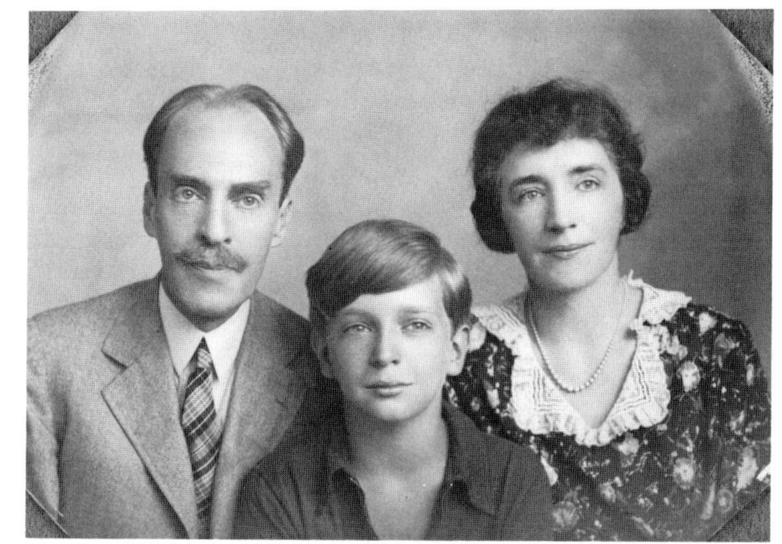

A passport photograph of Duncan, Laughlin, and myself taken just prior to our Giorgione trip in 1932.

The relationship with Duncan was inspiring and stimulating. He had such an intense interest, not just in my art but in the work of other artists as well. He was very encouraging. Some of my paintings he loved just as they were, but he couldn't resist making a suggestion sometimes. I didn't always follow his suggestions. Only if I agreed.

When I wanted complete privacy for painting, which I did need because otherwise I wouldn't have any style of my own, I would go into my studio at home and put a sign on my door that said "Please don't disturb," just like on a hotel bedroom door. The sign on my door worked. No one disturbed me. Not at that time, but they didn't like it. Mother used to get quite miffed when she would come to the house and see the sign. She would say: "Marjorie, what are you doing in your lair?" Duncan used to love to dash into the room pretending to look at the indoor-outdoor thermometer, and then he'd always try to see what I was doing.

After we moved out of our home on 21st Street in 1930 to our newly built home on Foxhall Road which we called "Dunmarlin" (a combination of Duncan, Marjorie, and Laughlin), the old house was given over completely to the museum and there was

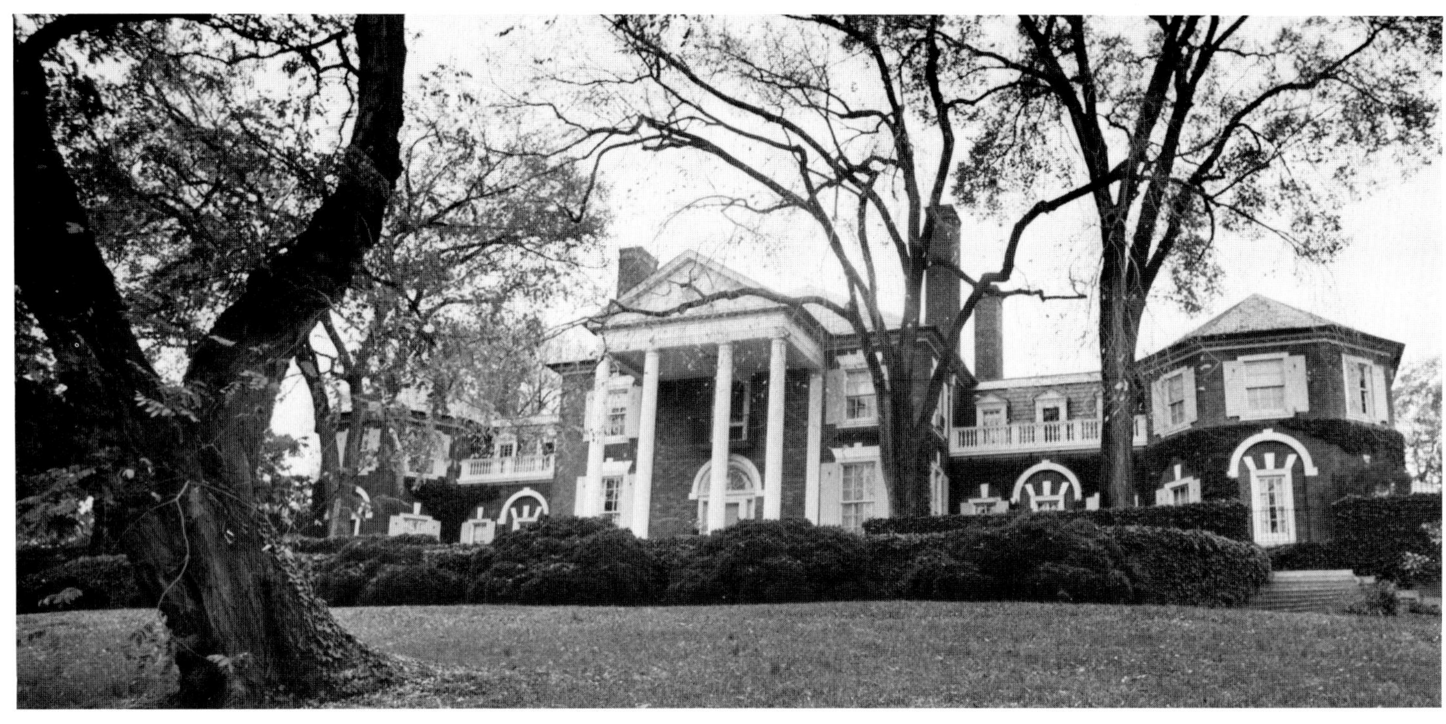

Our house on Foxhall Road.
PHOTO BY PAUL HOSEFROS

much more exhibition space. Duncan assigned an exhibition room for my paintings. The ones that we both admired, the ones that we both thought were best at the time, just seemed to drift over to that room. We didn't change all of the paintings in the room regularly, just a few at a time, adding one here and one there. As director, Duncan always supervised the hanging of my paintings, as well as the hanging of all the paintings throughout the building.

I was associate director of the museum from 1925 until Duncan's death in 1966. Most of the work was done with Duncan and it was all equally exciting: selecting paintings or prints to buy; discussing plans; travelling; meeting artists, critics, art dealers, museum directors, etc. I concentrated on the basement rooms. They were called the print rooms but there were paintings shown there too. My responsibility was to get up exhibitions for these rooms. Most of the exhibitions came from dealers in New York City. One that I remember particularly was the Rothko show from which we bought the painting *Green and Maroon*. Duncan took a great interest in everything I did.

Duncan died in 1966, and a few weeks after his death I started writing the book about him which was entitled *Duncan Phillips and His Collection*. I missed Duncan tremendously. He was such good company, so interesting. Writing the book saved me from suffering as much. I had to concentrate. I had to get it done, it was important. It took over two years and involved a lot of research.

From 1966 until 1972, I was director of The Phillips Collection, in accordance with Duncan's wishes. During that period the accomplishment that gave me greatest satisfaction was the loan exhibition of paintings by Paul Cézanne in honor of the fiftieth anniversary of the collection's opening. All in all about 83 paintings and drawings were on view. There were great crowds. People lined the street waiting to see it.

I was able to put on our first outdoor sculpture show because of the generous loan of a group of works from the Marlborough Galleries in New York. It was shown in the small sculpture court off the new wing and attracted enthusiastic attention. Sandy Calder came from New York to see that his large stabile was placed exactly as he wished.

Among the paintings and sculpture which I purchased with gallery funds during the period were works by Alicia Penalba, Sam Gilliam, Howard Mehring, Jack Youngerman, Cleve Gray, David Hare, Clyfford Still, and a mask head by Pablo Picasso.

In 1972 I retired as director of The Phillips Collection and our son Laughlin, who was president, became the new director. I had more time for painting.

In 1973 I received an honorary degree from Smith College, a Doctor of Fine Arts, as recognition of my work as director and also my work as a painter. I'll always remember the delightful surprise that took place after the awards ceremony and the dinner that followed at Smith College. Mrs. Griswold, wife of a former president of Yale, blindfolded me and turned me round and round. When she stopped and took off the blindfold, I found myself standing in front of my painting, *The Buzzard.* It was such a surprise. The painting had been brought over from Yale University for the occasion.

In 1975 my friend Carroll Purves (Mrs. Edmond R. Purves) and I went to France. After seeing mutual friends in Paris, we went to Saint Paul de Vence where the Fondation Maeght was opening a wonderful Bonnard retrospective exhibition which lasted from July 12th to September 28th. The Phillips Collection had loaned a favorite painting of mine, *The Open Window*, and we were happy to see how stunning it looked in the show.

It was the first time I had seen the fine building housing the paintings with its ample grounds displaying numerous examples of outstanding sculpture. Later we stayed for a banquet at the Maeght residence which also housed many fine contemporary paintings.

I asked the director, Mr. Pratt, if he could arrange a visit to Bonnard's home on the Riviera at Le Cannet which I had especially looked forward to seeing. It was after Bonnard's death. It turned out that Bonnard's nephew, Mr. Terrasse, and his wife were living there and would be delighted to have us come. I had met him in Washington when he generously loaned to Duncan Bonnard's great painting *The Old Horse* for a full year just because my husband loved it so and had found that it was not for sale. Duncan hung it in The Phillips Collection to the edification of many people, including ourselves!

When we arrived at the house we were welcomed cordially and shown all the rooms which the artist had made so famous. I felt especially privileged to see the studio. It was quite small and had a slanting skylight. A portion of the white latticed fence he used so often in his work was kept there and made one feel at home. Otherwise the room was empty. I did not see any palettes, which were perhaps already in the Louvre, and I was pleased to see that the walls were pink, exactly the same as in our dining room at home. Painted in layers of warm and cool. A perfect background for pictures of most any period.

I continued painting until 1982, when I worked on a series of orchids. One of the orchid paintings was done at the time of the terrible airplane accident at the Fourteenth Street Bridge near National Airport. I felt very sad, and it helped to paint. I hope some of my feeling of sorrow was reflected in the painting. I did not paint after that because of my eyes.

On my ninetieth birthday, my son Laughlin gave me a superb party at The Phillips Collection. So many friends and family were there, at least a hundred, and my granddaughter cut the cake. At the house there was another birthday cake, and I was pleased to have blown out all the candles. The accompanying photographs were taken around the time of my 90th birthday and include my dearly loved schnauzer, Pep II, and my niece, Sylvia Partridge, discussing the book with me.

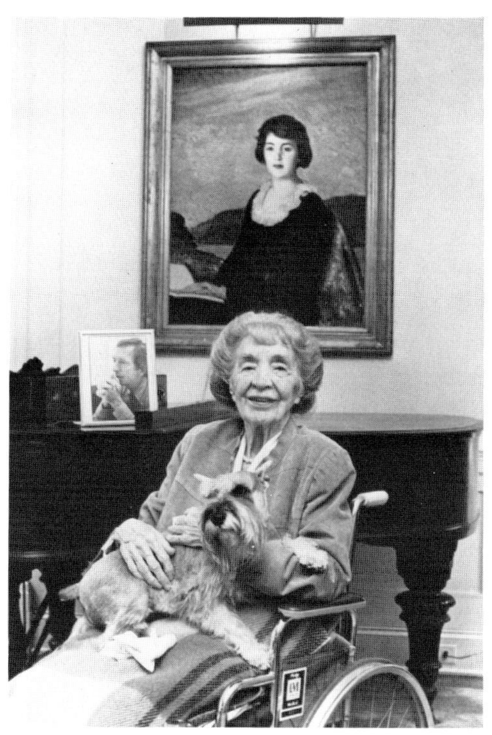

PHOTO BY BILL SNEAD—*The Washington Post*

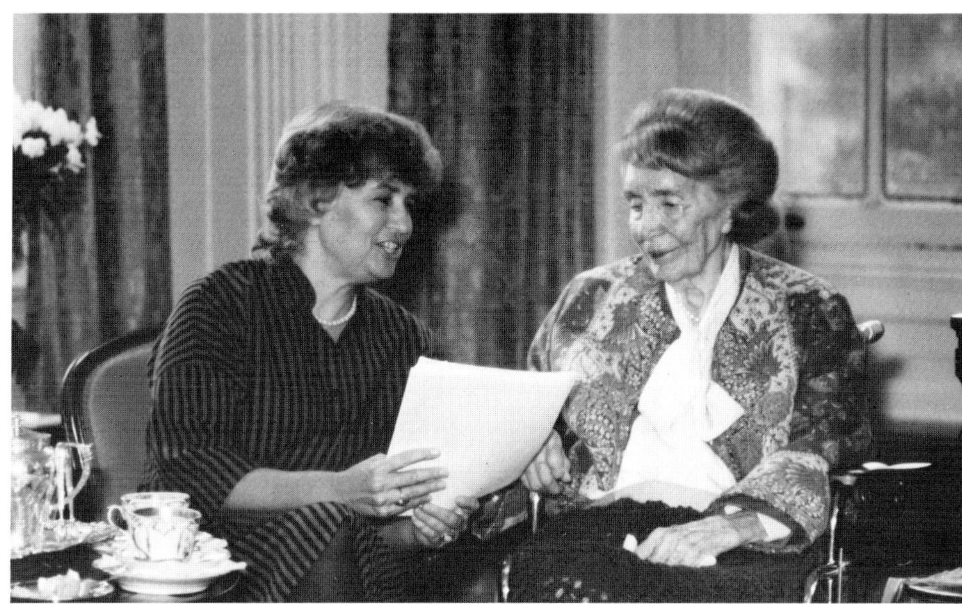

PHOTO BY RUTH BOLDUAN

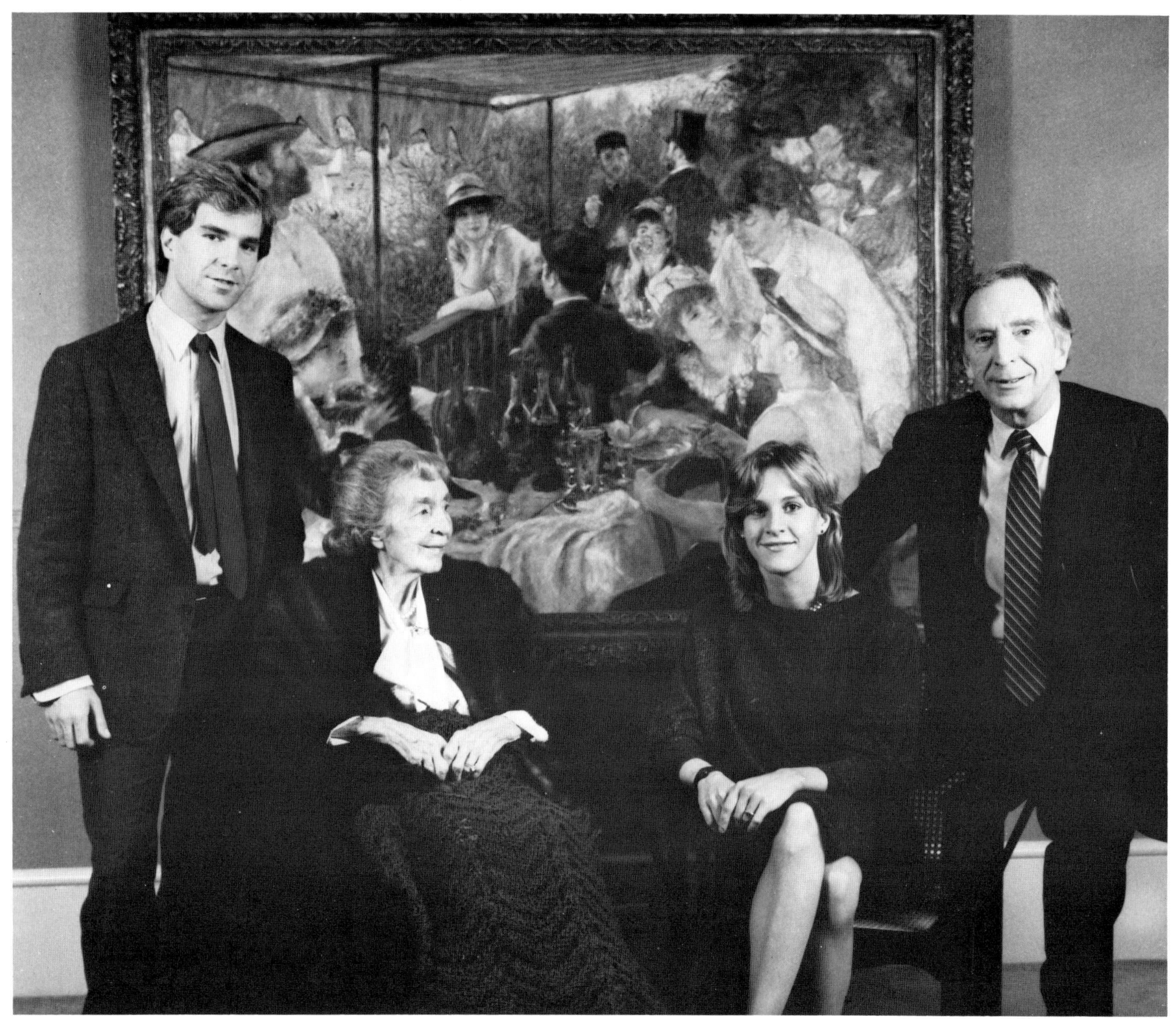

Left to right: my grandson Duncan Vance Phillips, myself, my granddaughter Liza Phillips, and my son Laughlin Phillips in front of the great masterpiece 'Luncheon of the Boating Party' by Renoir.
PHOTO BY RUTH BOLDUAN

COLOR PLATES AND COMMENTS

THE HUDSON AT OSSINING (Marjorie Acker)
c. 1920. Oil on canvas, 18 × 24 inches
The Phillips Collection, Washington, D.C.

One of the most thrilling days of my life was when Duncan purchased this painting just two days after we first met. It meant the world to me because I admired his "eye" for art so very much. The painting shows the broad expanse of the Hudson River which I loved so much. In the foreground numerous little boats were docked unobtrusively. Across the river was Croton Point, a fascinating feature to me.

At Croton itself there lived many artists and intellectuals. Young Sandy (Alexander) Calder was one who was outstandingly original. He eventually changed the course of American sculpture to come. We knew the family well and delighted in their independence and originality. Sandy's sister, Peggy, went to Miss Fuller's School with us and we still feel very close although she lives in Berkeley, California. She maintains the "art" of letter writing.

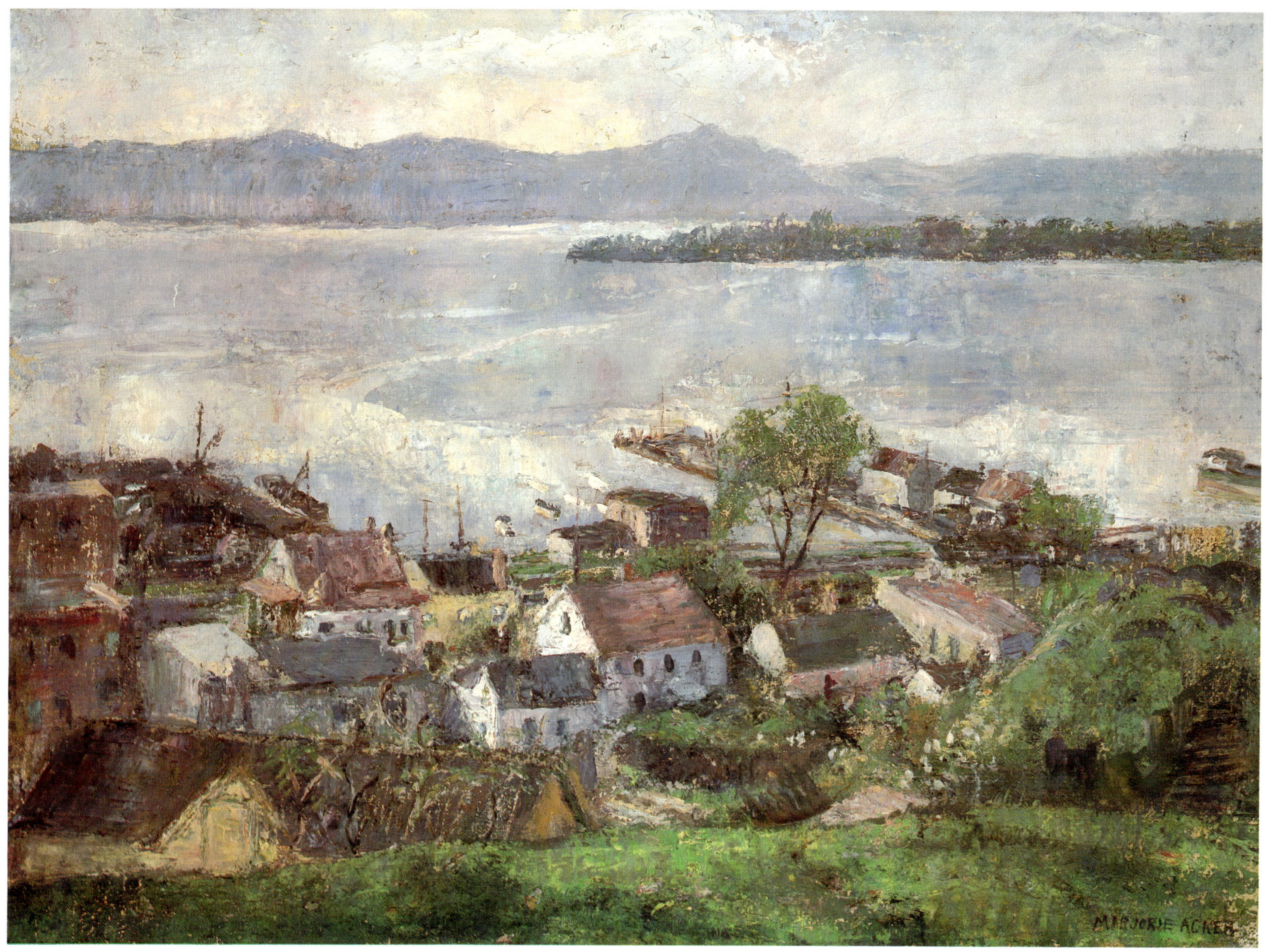
MARJORIE ACKER

AN EDGE OF AUNT MARY'S GARDEN (Marjorie Acker)

c. 1920. Oil on canvas, 22 × 36 inches
Estate of the Artist

Aunt Mary's garden . . . the general aspect of it was going into a world of delight. It was at "Wilellyn," my grandparents Beals' summer home in Newburgh, New York, and was designed by a landscape architect named Louis Brown in the shape of a wheel with spokes radiating out from the center. The spokes were the various flower beds, and at the center was a sundial. There were so many delights . . . a bust of Homer, etc. Aunt Mary experimented with many different kinds of flowers. She had a lot of roses and larkspur. The garden was a great influence on me because it was so imaginative. I spent lots of time there in the summers. It always seemed to give me some inspiration.

An Edge of Aunt Mary's Garden was painted at the end of one of the spokes of the wheel. There was a fountain and a pool and the bust of Homer, the great Greek poet, who is being crowned with laurel leaves in the painting just as we often did. The people portrayed are imaginary, although they could be my sister Eleanor and myself and my little brother William. The painting reveals just some of the many charms of that garden, some of the surprise aspects. At the other end of the garden was a small, lovely marble bench where Duncan and I became engaged, and at the terminal end was a great big curved bench which led to the climax of the huge ancient apple tree with powerful boughs that we children used to climb.

Aunt Mary's bedroom was beautiful too. It was all in pink, with a lovely draped dressing table—all of the things that people admired in those days. She had quite an artistic sense. Once when I asked my mother, who was unusually independent in her judgments, what she thought of a newly acquired painting by Bonnard, she said "I'll have to ask my sister Mary."

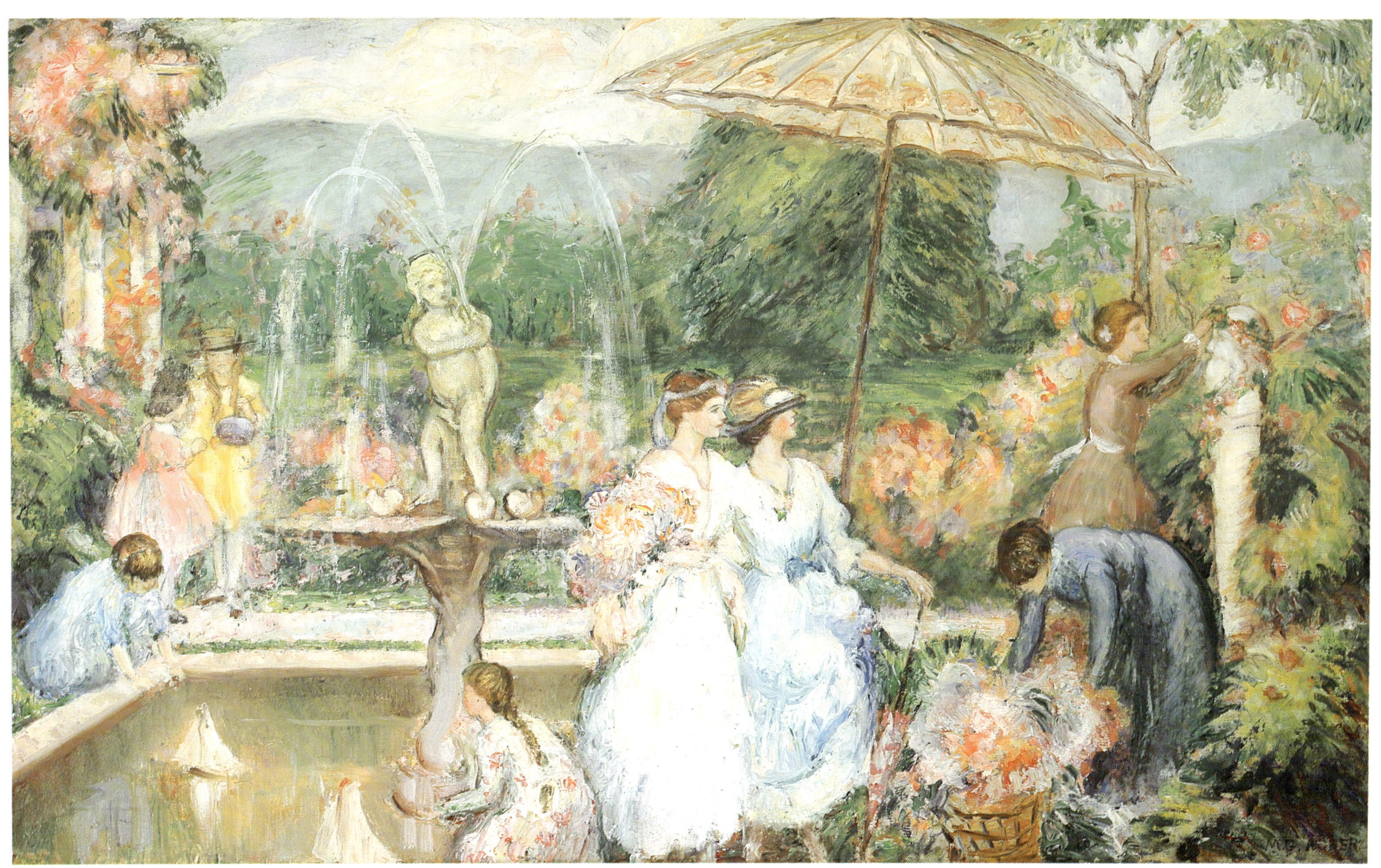

NUNS ON THE ROOF

1922. Oil on canvas, 24¼ × 22 inches
The Phillips Collection, Washington, D.C.

Duncan and I lived in New York for two months during the first year we were married. His kindly cousin Leila and her husband, Lister Carlisle, lent us their beautiful apartment during the time when they were in Florida that year. Duncan wrote and visited the galleries, and I had the pleasure of often painting from the windows. This painting, *Nuns on the Roof*, I particularly enjoyed doing. The color is delicate but the buildings are substantial and build up to a stately composition. I was surprised to see the nuns walking there just across the street.

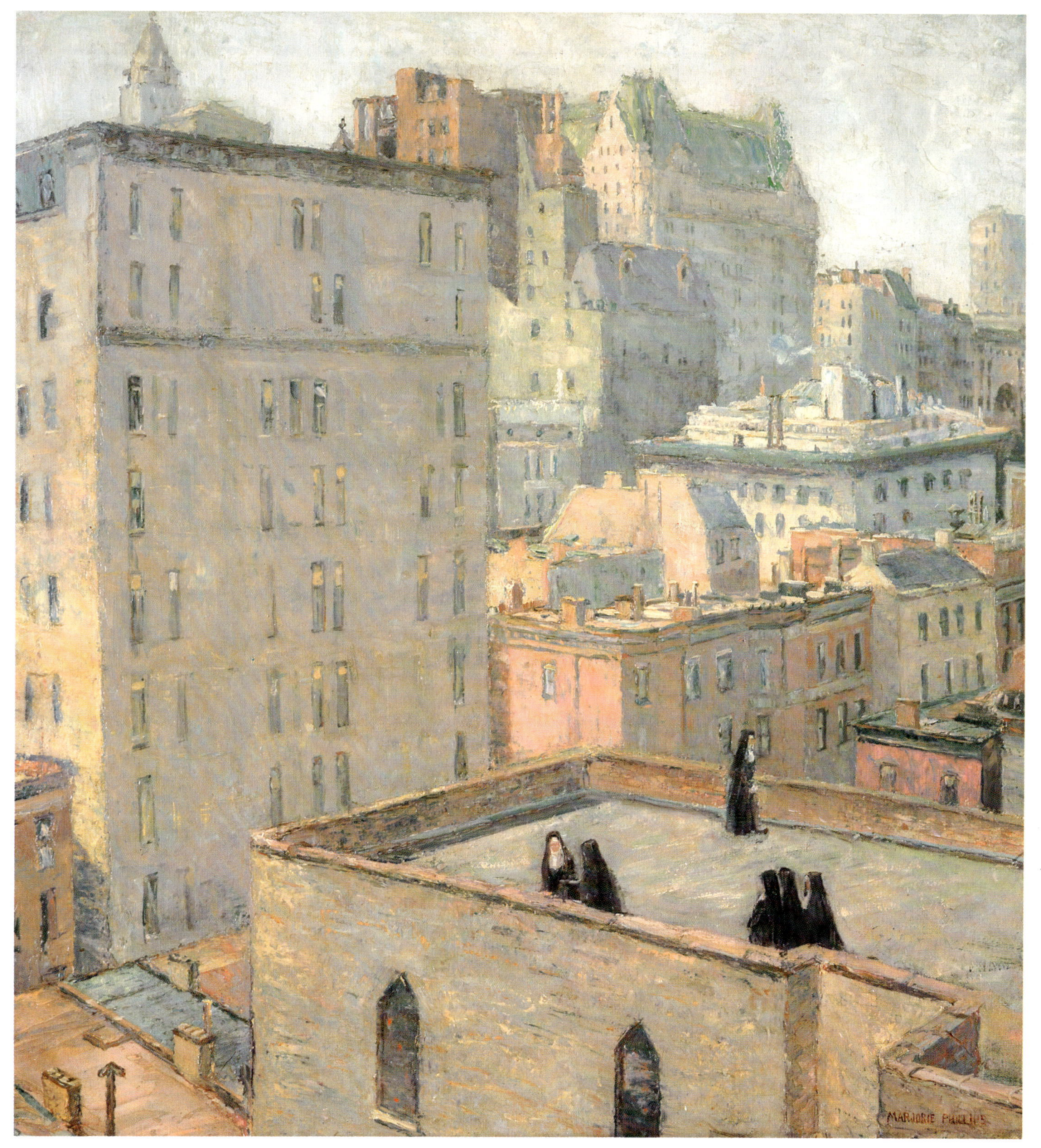
MARJORIE PHILLIPS

RUE DE LA BOETIE

1923. Oil on canvas board, 9½ × 12½ inches
The Phillips Collection, Washington, D.C.

This was painted on the trip to Paris in 1923, the same trip on which we purchased Renoir's *The Luncheon of the Boating Party.* Of course I had my paint box along and had a chance to do several small paintings.

Duncan and I and Mary Marjorie were staying at a hotel called Le Gallais in Paris. I used to be charmed at watching the traffic on the Rue de la Boetie and painted this from the hotel window using the "petite couteau." I remember how noisy the traffic was in those days, with the horns tooting and the horses clattering by.

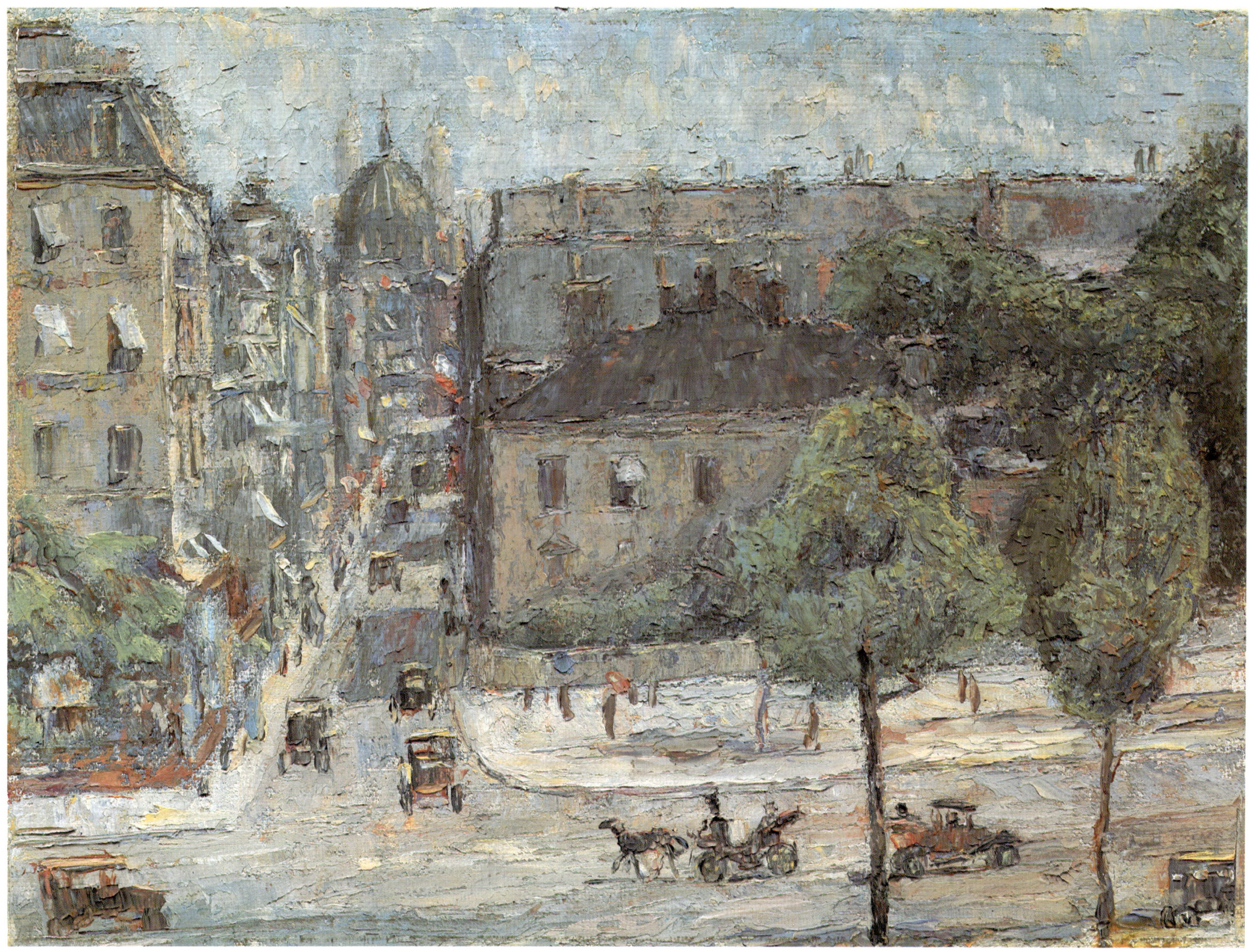

BEFORE SUPPER

c. 1925. Oil on canvas, 20⅛ × 19⅝ inches
Laughlin Phillips, Washington, D.C.

When I was painting in my studio in Ebensburg, Pennsylvania, during the summers, I used to look out the window and see the children with their nurse. It was a great pleasure to know that I could keep watch on them while they were playing outside and make sure that they were doing well. This was the scene exactly as I saw it from my studio window that day, and many other days. It must have been shortly before five in the afternoon, since the children had their supper at five. There was already a glow in the sky.

Here Laughlin must be about one and Mary Marjorie about three. Laughlin's nurse is sitting on the left. She was a very calm person and a bit stolid, lost in her own thoughts. She was probably knitting something for the children. The girl on the pony is one of the chauffeur John's daughters. She grew up to become a stewardess and then married well—a naval officer, I believe. The pony is the same pony that Mary Marjorie was riding in the painting *Summer Morning*.

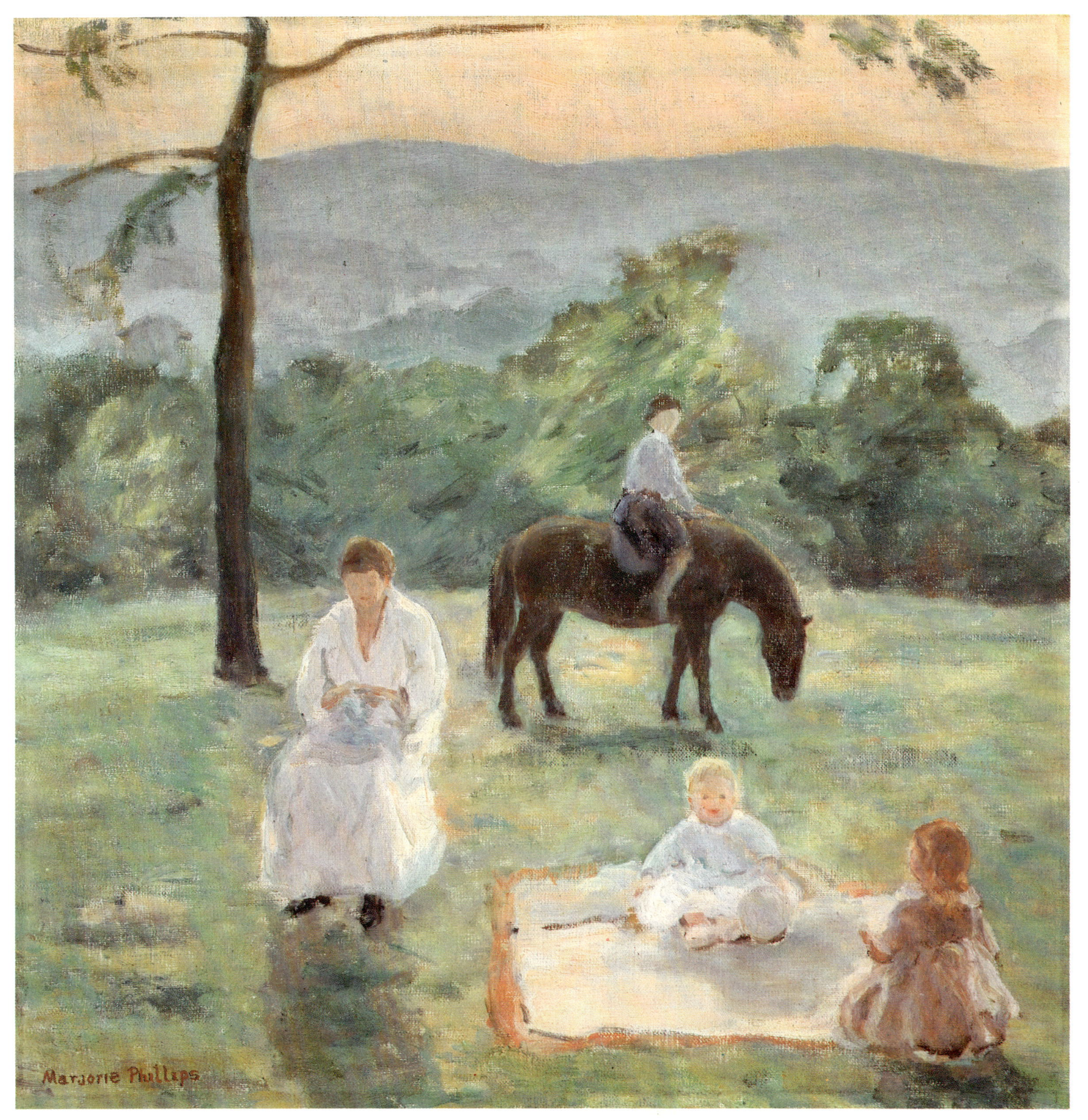
Marjorie Phillips

BREAKFAST ROOM

c. 1925. Oil on canvas, 24 × 30 inches
The Phillips Collection, Washington, D.C.

This was our daily breakfast. Duncan and I and the children always had breakfast together in a room on the third floor of the house that's now The Phillips Collection. We occupied the third floor and Mother Phillips had the entire second floor to herself.

In this painting our daughter Mary Marjorie must be about five and Laughlin about three. The dog was Duncan's dog, an airedale. Duncan used to take him out in Rock Creek Park and let him run without a leash, but he'd always come back. I believe that's the old Walsh-McLean house outside the window.

Ages ago, when this painting was shown at the Bignou Gallery in New York City, a friend said in a shocked voice, "Why, Marjorie, your hair is down!" Isn't that funny? Some people were so stiff then. To her it was very daring to paint myself with my hair down. Now it wouldn't matter at all. It was just natural for me to do it.

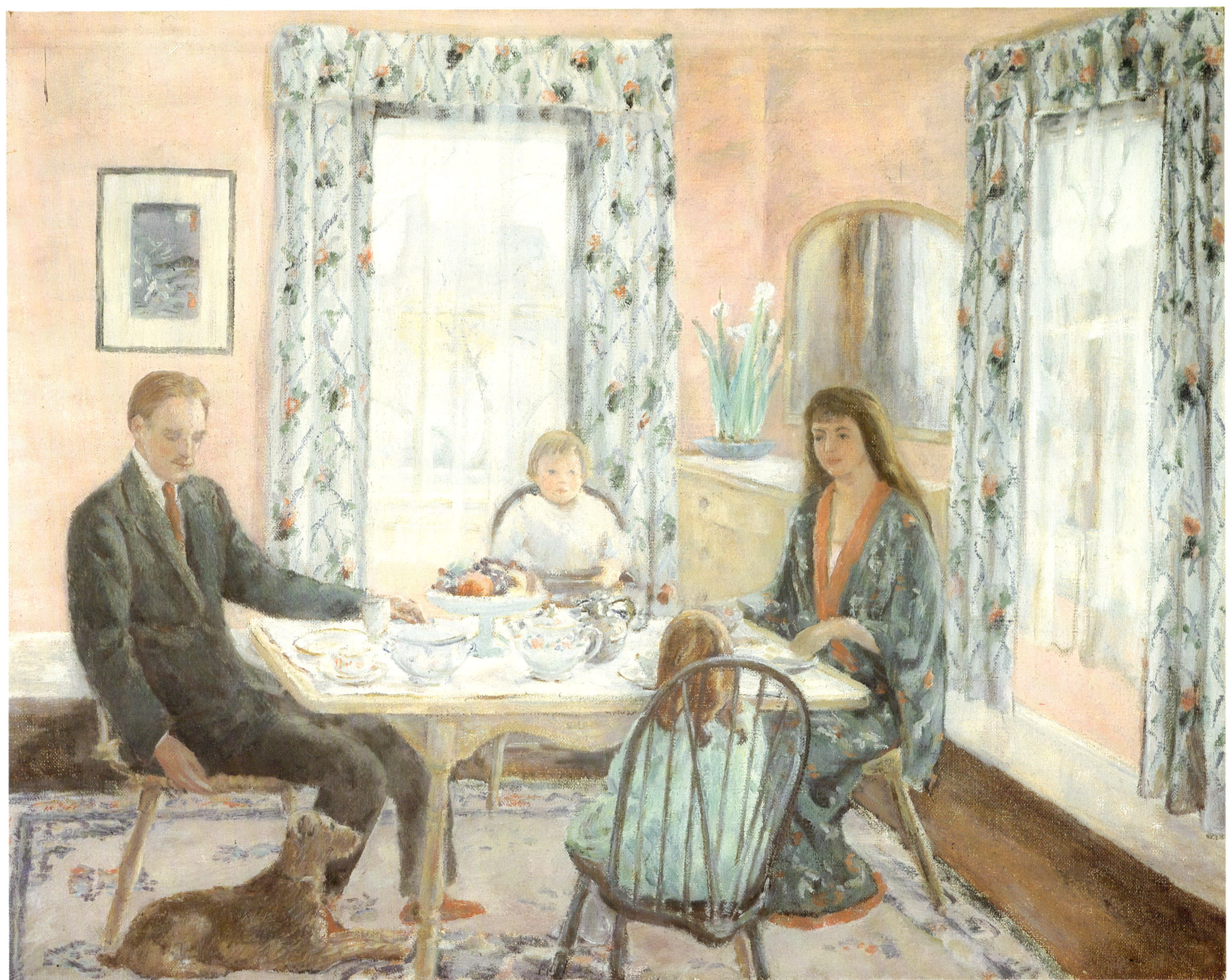

POPPIES

1925. Oil on canvas, 23 ⅞ × 17 ⅞ inches
Mr. and Mrs. Anthony Hope, Washington, D.C.

Flowers are so varied and have such life and beautiful colors, such a variety of color and shapes. They've always been a joy. I've tried to get that life, that extreme life, that flowers innately have. They pass it on to you. Very often I've missed, but sometimes I've been able to pass it on through a painting that's successful.

Poppies was painted outside my studio in Ebensburg in the pergola. I had to work fast so the flowers wouldn't fade. It probably took me two mornings. The fallen petal is important in the painting. It gives a slight contrast.

I've tried to stress simplification in this painting, simplifying the form. I had been reading Clive Bell's book in which he used the phrase "transpose before nature," meaning to give the subject artistic form, to give it vitality. This had great meaning for me.

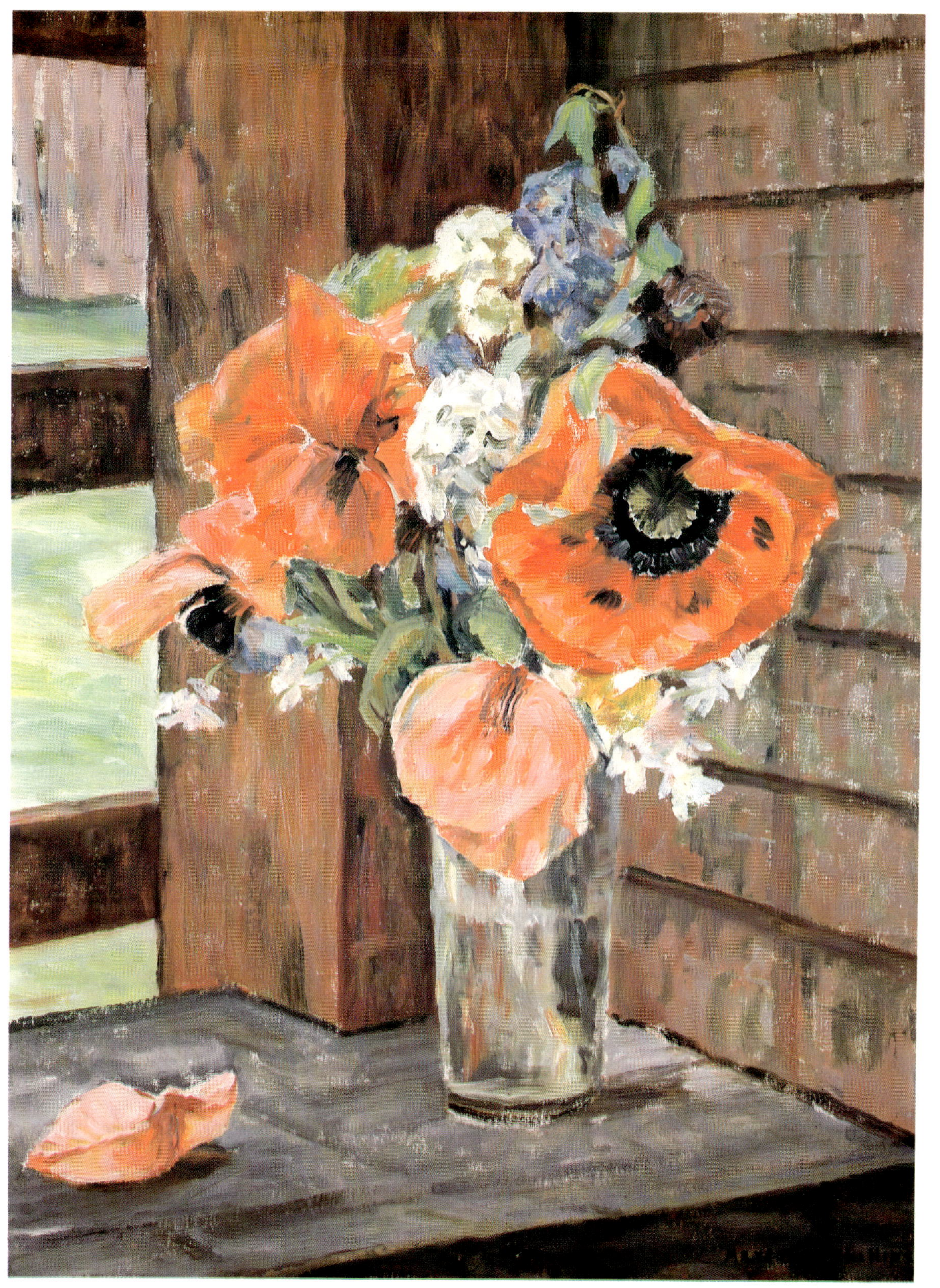

SUMMER MORNING

c. 1925. Oil on canvas, 30⅛ × 35⅞ inches
Jennifer Phillips, Washington, D.C.

When I was a schoolgirl, I was sitting in my room one day trying to do my homework and my brother William was there talking every minute. William was a tremendous talker and he didn't require many answers, so I had learned to think my own thoughts as he talked on and on. I got quite dextrous. It was then that I decided to paint the celebration of the wonder of the world. I didn't want to paint depressing pictures. There were so many depressing things; so many self-conscious, forced, foolish things. That's why my paintings are all on the cheerful side—I felt it was needed. There are the two sides, but it's hard to get in everything.

Summer Morning is a little celebration, a little procession. At that time, Mary Marjorie loved to sit on the back of a horse. This is the path to my studio in Ebensburg, our summer home. Many of the Phillips family had houses in this area, although we didn't see them very much. Our summers were quiet. Duncan did his writing and played golf, and I painted in the mornings. In the afternoons I took walks or joined the golf. I used to give little parties for the children. I loved the idea of celebrating.

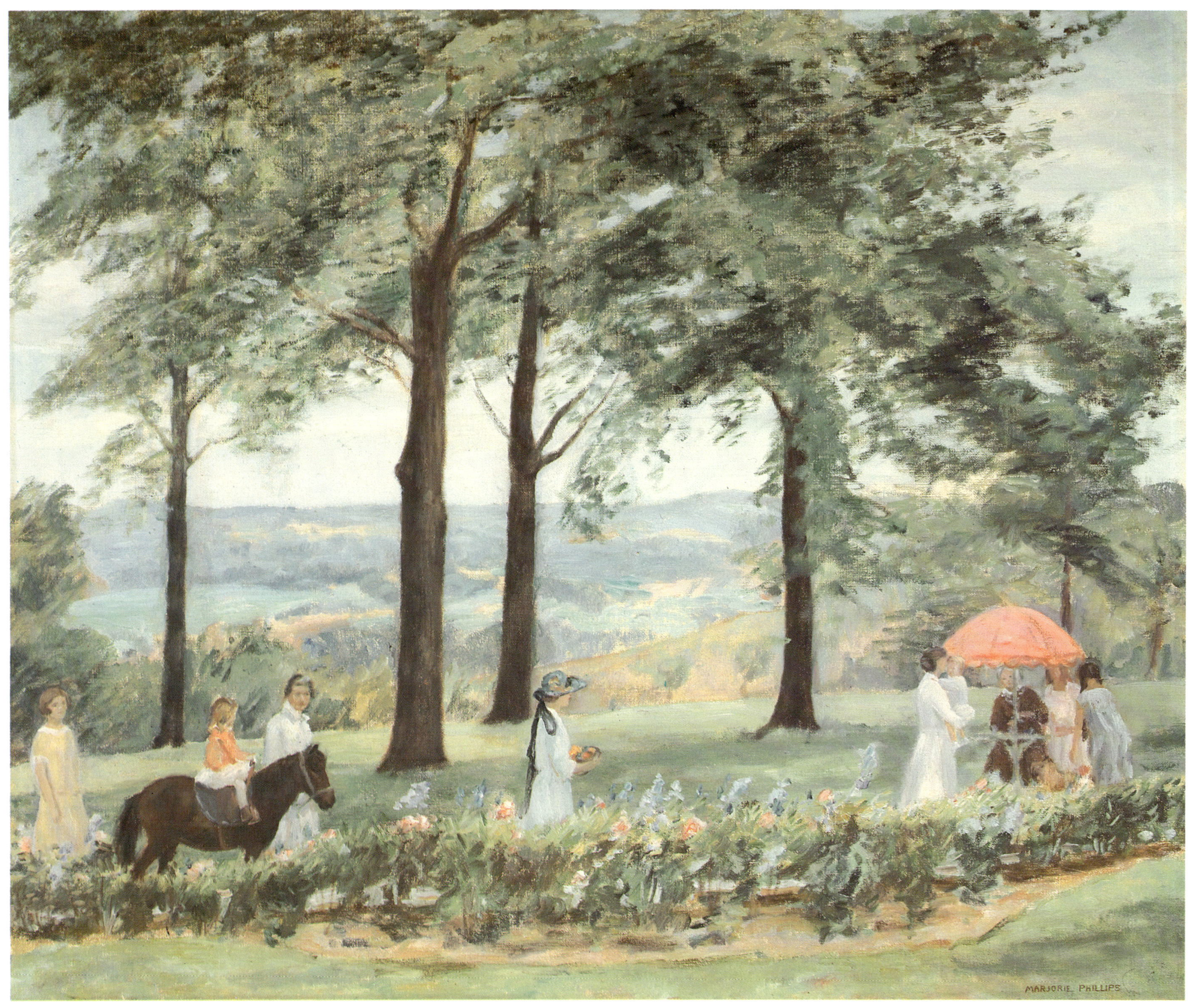
MARJORIE PHILLIPS

MAYPOLE

c. 1927–28. Oil on canvas, 26 × 34 inches
The Phillips Collection, Washington, D.C.

The landscape for this painting was done not far from our home in Ebensburg. After driving out with the chauffeur, I worked sitting in our car which was parked in the field. At the end of the day, as we started to drive back home, we suddenly came to a protected hollow in the ground where a bootlegger was brewing his wares. He looked out in fury thinking that we were spying on him. He glowered and shook his fist. I was really scared and did not return to that place again.

The main interest, the maypole, was painted in nostalgic memory of when I felt as young as the children I made it for. I used to give maypole parties for my younger brothers and sisters. We would make the maypole ourselves—a long staff with a ring around the top and ribbons coming out from the ring. The children would dance around the maypole and get all tangled up. It was just a poetic idea.

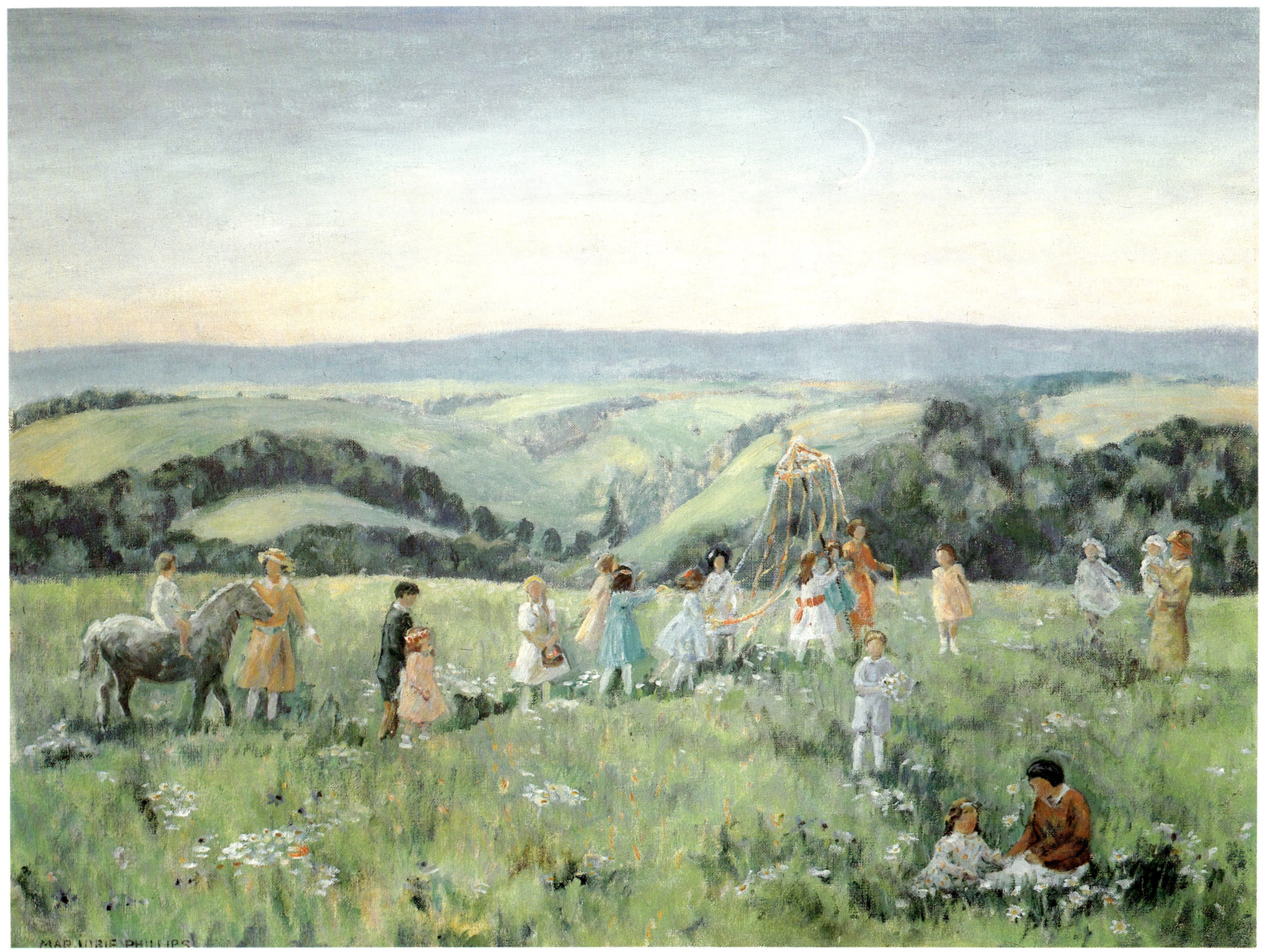
MARJORIE PHILLIPS

COCOANUT GROVE

c. 1930. Oil on canvas, 19 ½ × 23 ¼ inches
Estate of the Artist

At the invitation and insistence of one of Duncan's cousins, Duncan and I took a trip to Palm Beach, Florida, where we stayed at a big old wooden hotel with straw carpeting, The Royal Poinciana. My sister Eleanor came down from her home in New York and joined us. One evening we went to a nightclub nearby for a late dinner and the minstrel show.

I thoroughly enjoyed the nightclub. It was so different from anything we usually did or have done since. So colorful. The minstrels cracked jokes as well as danced. They were so good. That night I did a sketch for this painting, and then did the actual painting in our hotel room. I think you can see how much I enjoyed it.

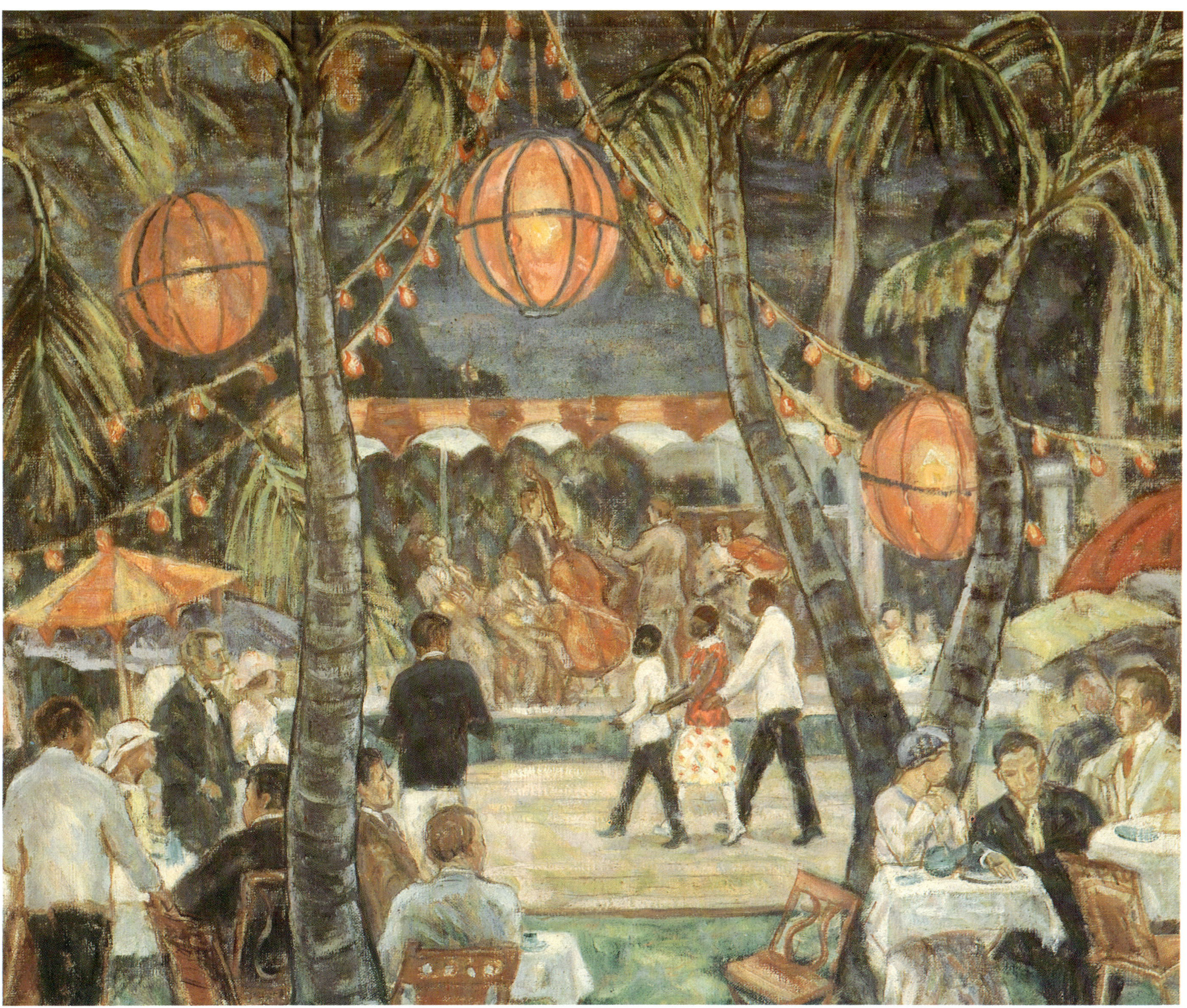

LITTLE BOUQUET

1934. Oil on canvas, 15 ½ × 14⅛ inches
The Phillips Collection, Washington, D.C.

I picked these flowers myself from our place in Ebensburg. This particular bouquet was in memory of the small bouquets that my Grandmother Beal used to make from Aunt Mary's garden. She would always have some roses and forget-me-nots and some lemon verbena. So much of my joy in painting seemed to go back to that garden. It touched my imagination in such a significant way. The picture was painted in the summer house outdoors. I thought that a grey background would have more charm than a landscape background because it would be less distracting.

My mother thought that this painting was very fine and had a lot of style. She thought it was the best thing I ever did, and that nothing after that ever quite measured up to it. Duncan also loved this painting and was responsible for a color reproduction in *Vanity Fair*. This is one of my most widely exhibited paintings.

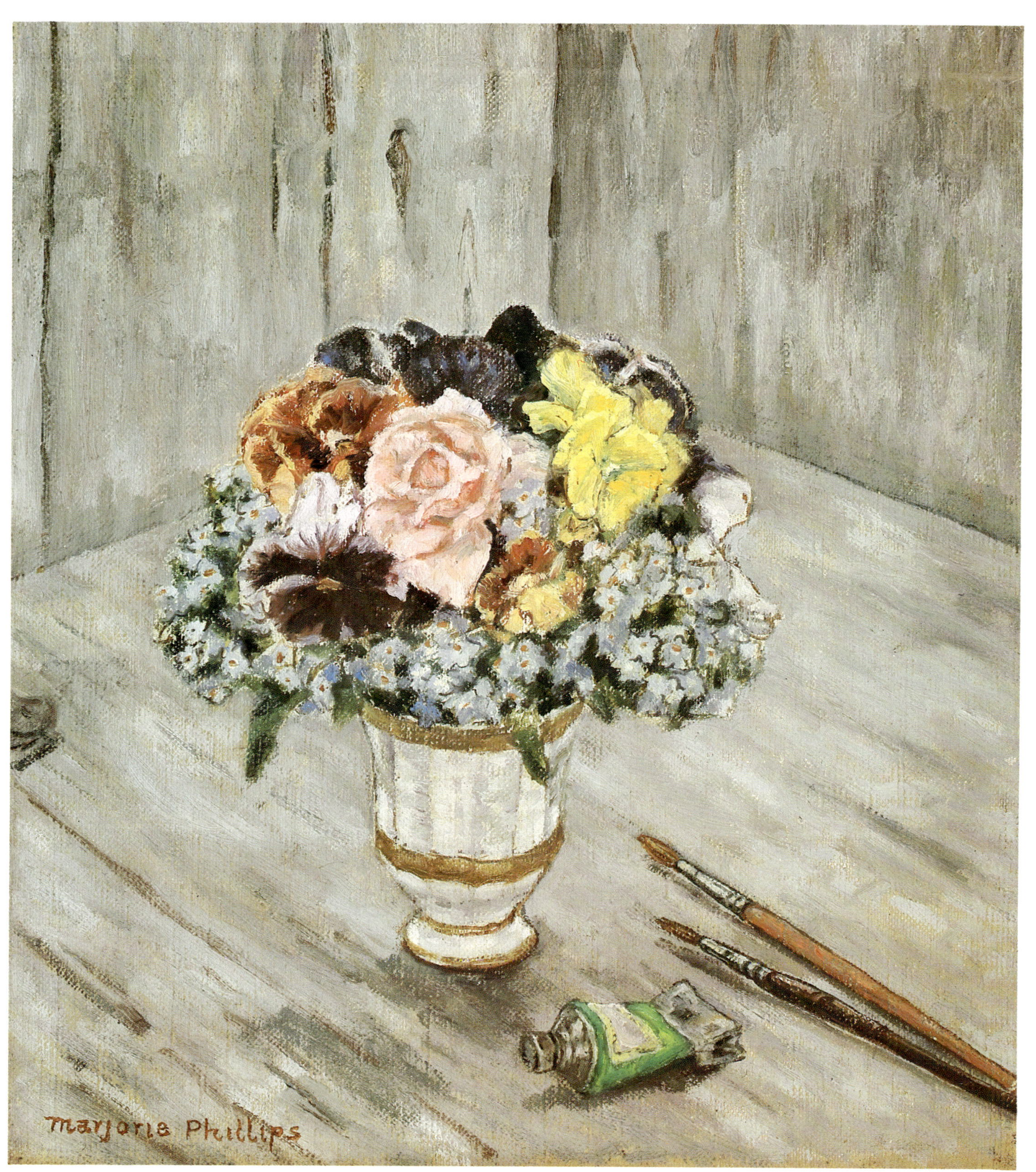
Marjorie Phillips

LOCUST TREES IN SPRING

1935. Oil on canvas, 23 × 40 inches
The Phillips Collection, Washington, D.C.

Every form of growth has a special character. Some forms you love and have a great respect for as I certainly had for these locust trees which were always very alive to me, very important in my life. They have been on the property since we first moved to our house in Washington, D.C., on Foxhall Road in 1930. It means a lot to look down and see them—so vigorous and strong and ancient as well as decorative. The trunks of the trees make a nice pattern. They seem to have so much stamina in order to live so long and be such a beautiful shape. I'm sure that the biggest one is nearing one hundred years old.

I always delighted in the view, just to use an everyday word—the Potomac River, the spires of Georgetown University, and the Fourteenth Street Bridge. I wanted to get an accurate feeling in the painting of my impression when I would look out.

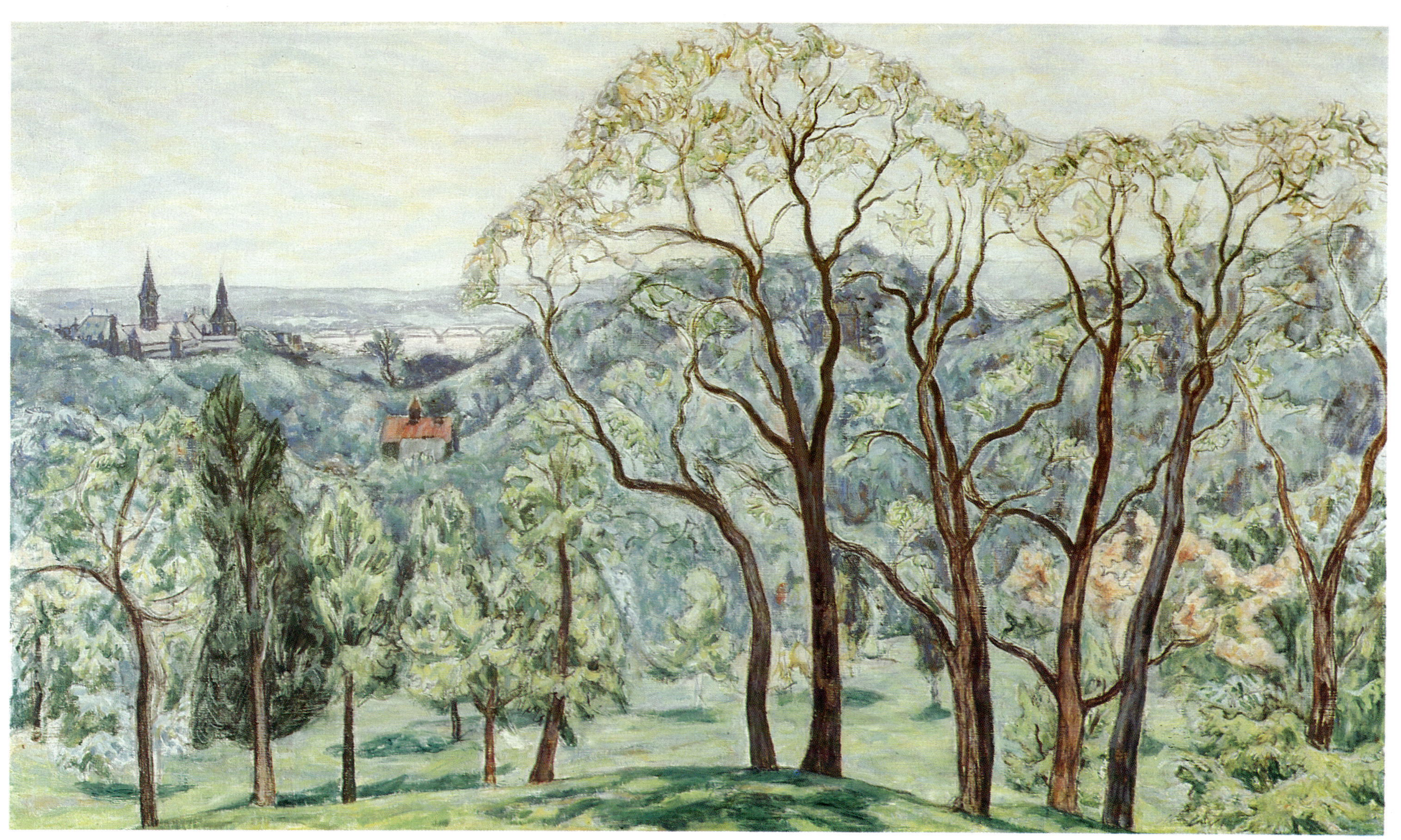

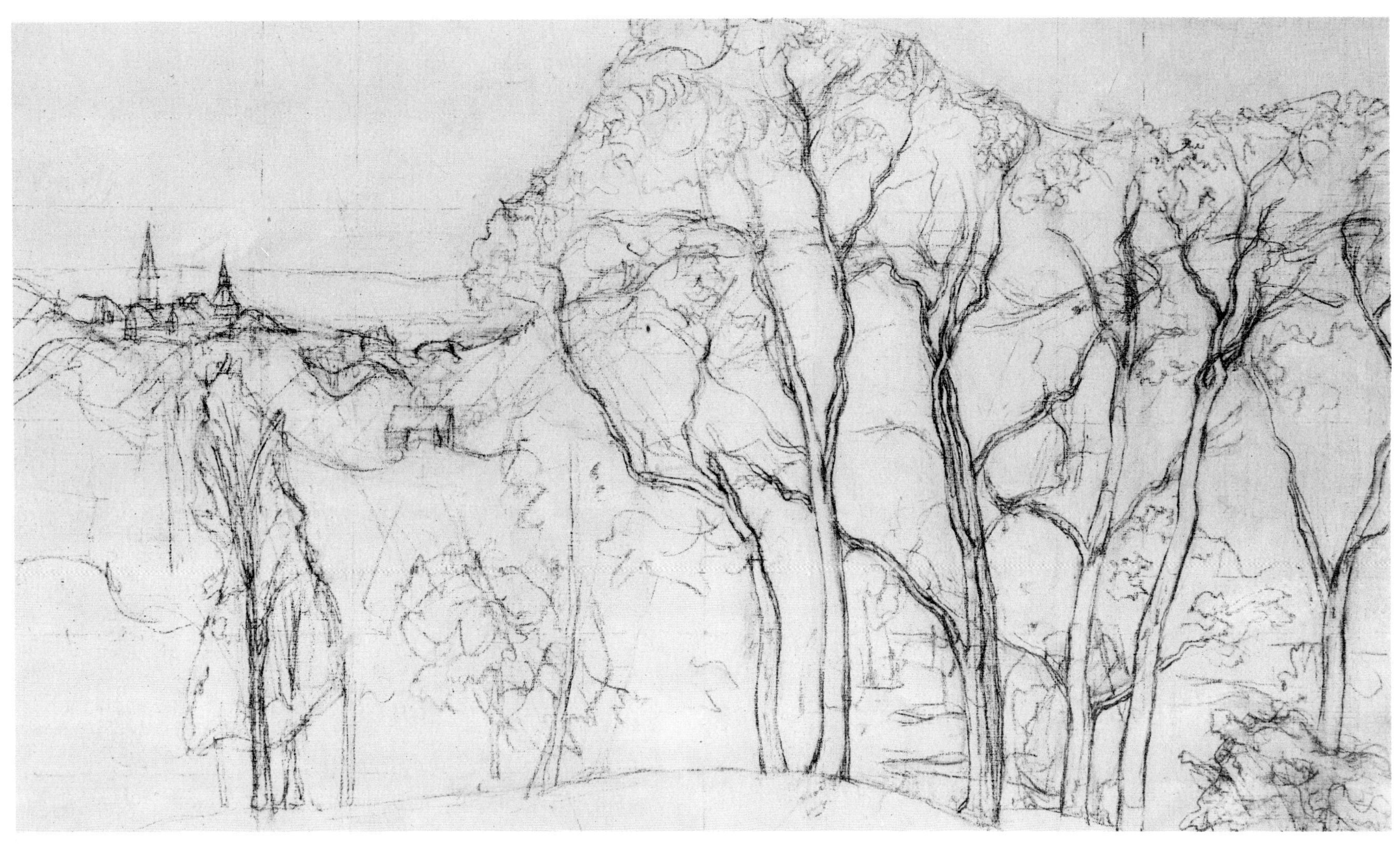

Drawing for *Locust Trees in Spring*, 1935

FOLLOWING PAGE:

WOODS AND FARMS

c. 1938. Oil on canvas, 25¼ × 80 inches
The Phillips Collection, Washington, D.C.

One day when my husband and I were driving along the road from Ebensburg to Cresson Springs, Pennsylvania, we saw this lovely rolling landscape with planted fields and crops against the distant Alleghenies. The hills were patterned by woods and farms so typical of that part of the country, but this was more enchanting than usual and I longed to paint it. I made a hurried study in wash and later did the painting itself in my studio in Ebensburg.

When we returned to Washington, *Woods and Farms* proved to be a good overmantel for Duncan's study. Later we used it in the dining room for the same purpose where it looked especially well against that subtle pink wall composed of layers of warm and cool paint which proved to be so perfect as a background for paintings. As I noted, this was the same pink that I later saw in Bonnard's studio during my visit to Le Cannet.

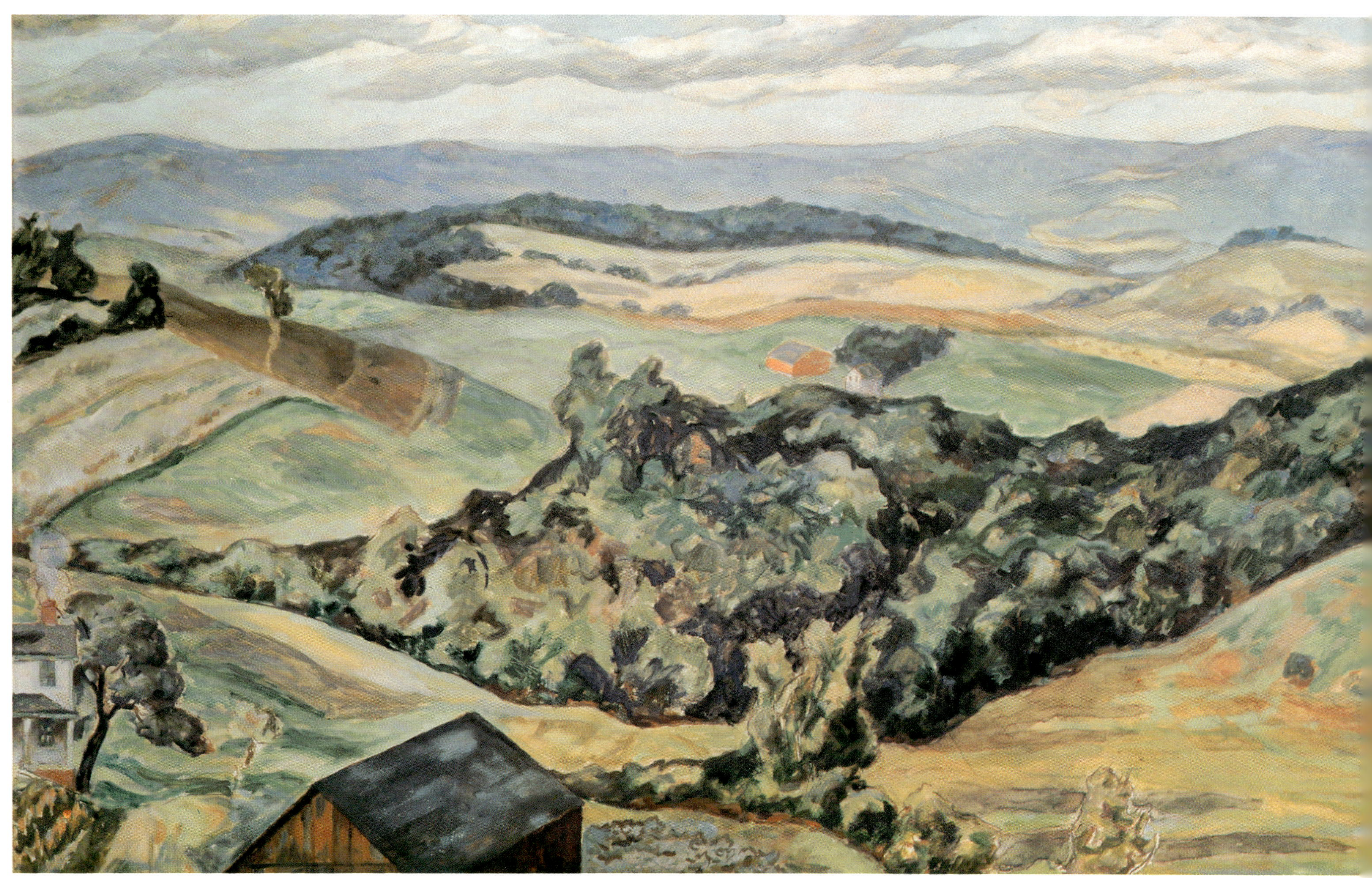

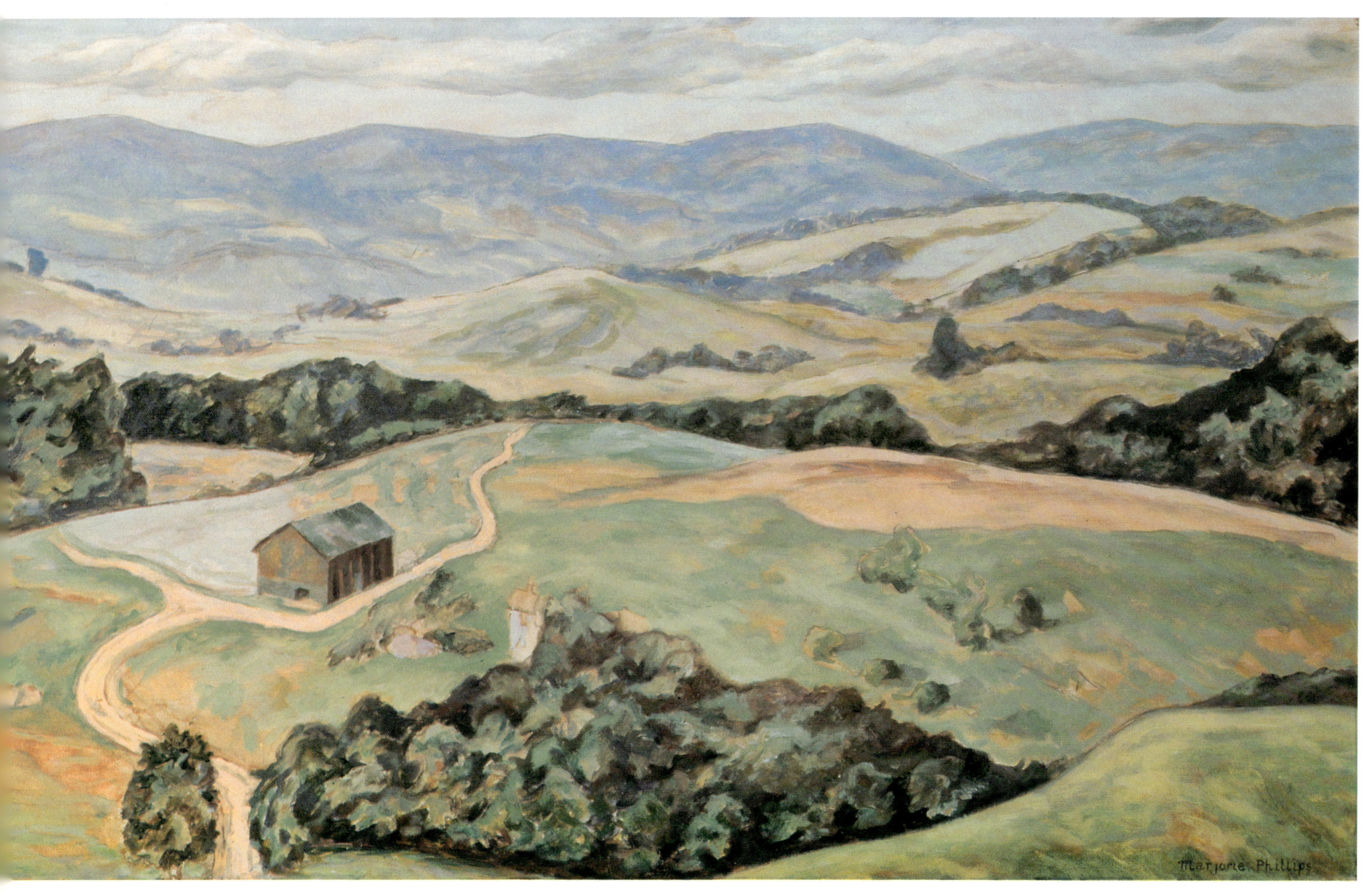
Marjorie Phillips

BASKET OF GRAPES

1939. Oil on canvas, 13¾ × 18¼ inches
Liza Phillips, Washington, D.C.

I painted this for Duncan because he loved Concord grapes so much. I tried to render the grapes in clusters, rather than painting them grape by grape, in order to get a bigger feeling. The peach is not too colorful so that it won't detract from the basket of grapes.

I always loved the shape of those baskets in which the fruit comes. They turn such wonderful colors. The knife looks good and sharp.

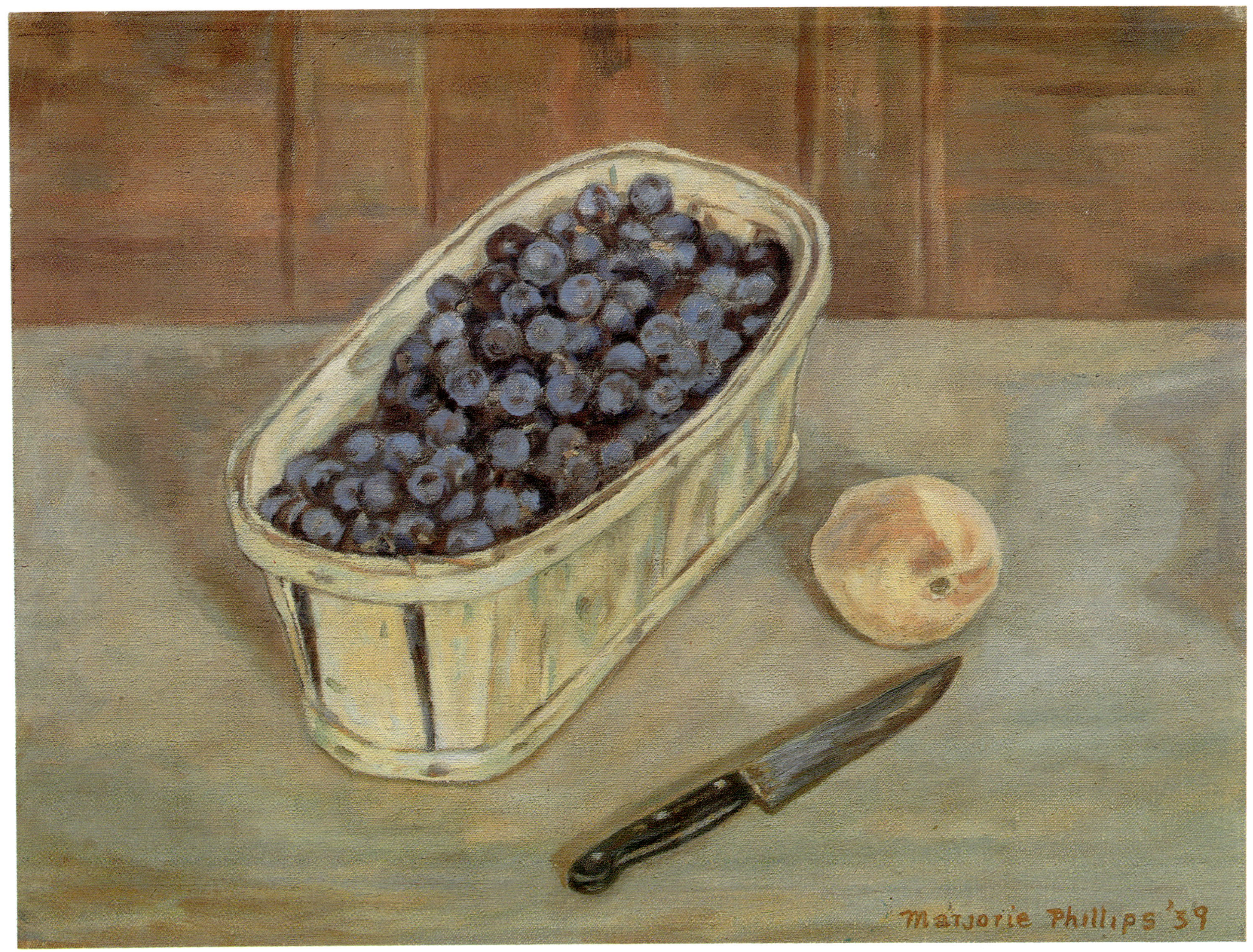
Marjorie Phillips '39

MORNING WALK

c. 1932. Oil on canvas, 22 × 36¼ inches
The Phillips Collection, Washington, D.C.

This was painted just after you got out of the pergola that was outside my studio in Ebensburg. It was done over the hedge. The road led to a hotel that a friend of Duncan's built to get his friends up from Pittsburgh to play golf. They all had a wonderful time. There was a band, and they used to have hayrides. The little white house was the gardener's house.

The two figures are myself and Mademoiselle. Mademoiselle was Laughlin's governess. She was French, and it was the time of the Lindbergh baby kidnapping. There was an epidemic of kidnapping after that. She would take Laughlin walking and hold his hand the entire time to make sure he was safe. She posed for this painting out in the burning sun. The spaniel was named Jeff. He was very attached to me and always followed me wherever I went, like a train following a locomotive. I couldn't get free of him.

I experimented quite a lot with what was called the "petite couteau," the "little palette knife," and you can see some of the effects in this painting on the right hand side. I definitely was trying to give it life. At that time there was a lot of talk about "keeping the picture plane." Instead of everything going off, it widens out and is corrected by a vertical.

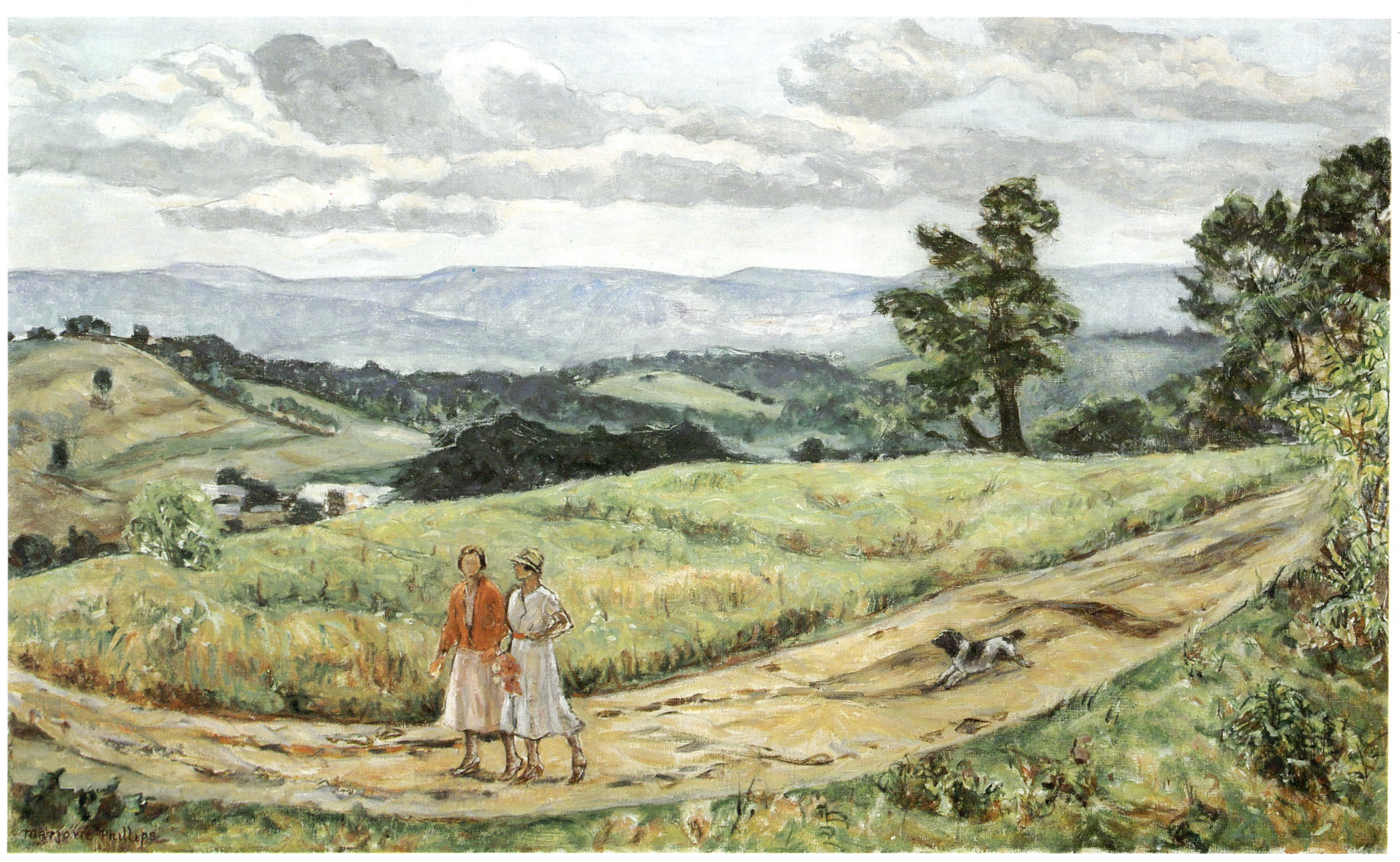
marjorie Phillips

BASKET OF PEACHES

c. 1943. Oil on canvas, 19⅞ × 16 inches
Gifford Phillips, New York, New York

I think peaches are very paintable. They have such wonderful subtle tones. I'd rather paint them than eat them. The fruit baskets often turn with time to the most beautiful subtle grey tones with the original yellow showing through, and I thought that this basket would be stunning with the peaches.

The painting was done in 1943 at Ebensburg in the downstairs bedroom which I sometimes used as a studio in rainy weather. Laughlin and Jim McLaughlin, the curator at The Phillips Collection and a good friend, used to paint there also. It was before Duncan had started to paint. It's a very simple design. The background is imaginary. I tried to have the colors harmonious, bringing them out to their full value. I'm glad to see how the darks count.

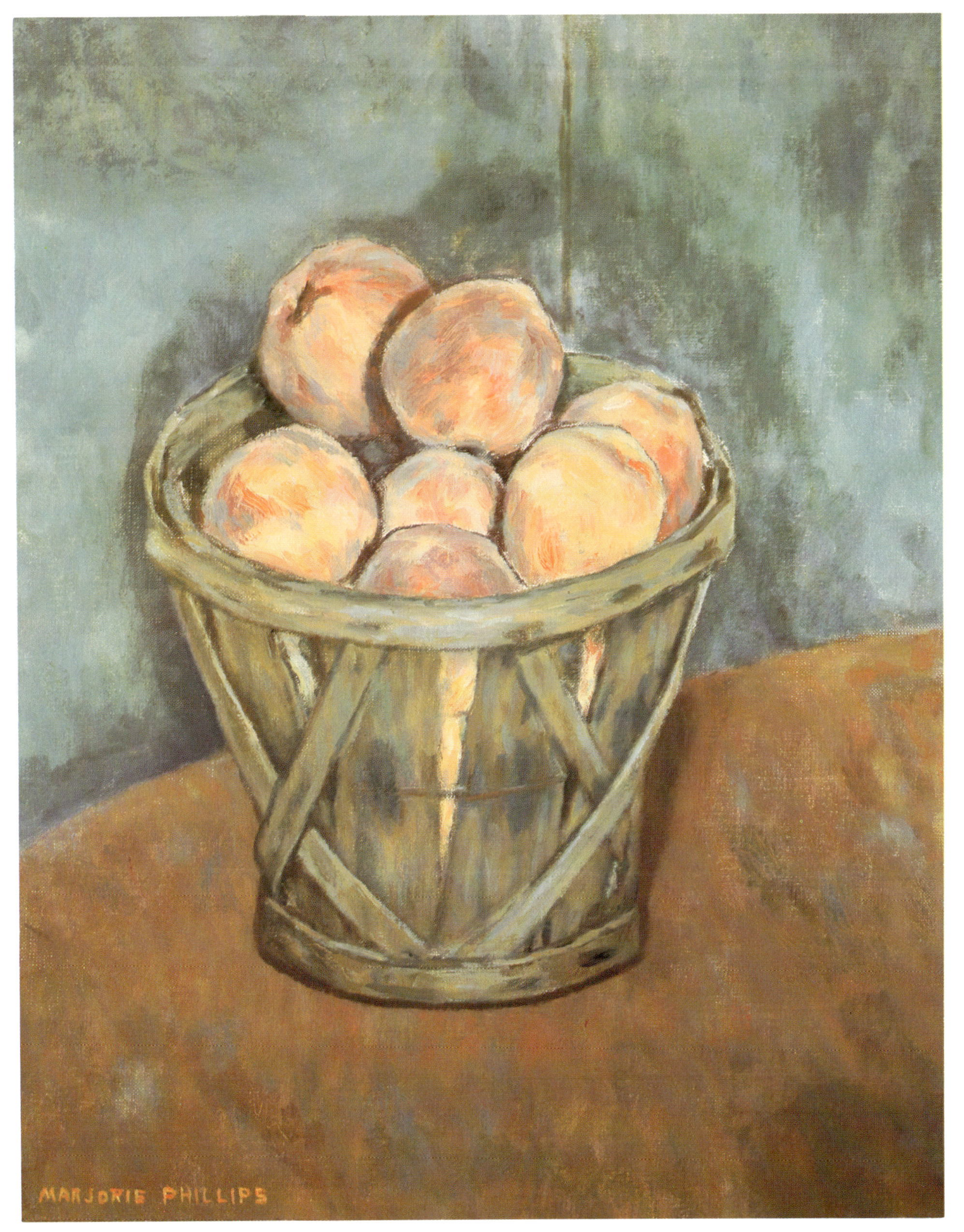
MARJORIE PHILLIPS

BIG BARN ON A HILL

c. 1943. Oil on canvas, $22\frac{7}{8} \times 28$ inches
Duncan V. Phillips, New York, New York

This barn must have been the idol of its owners because it was so colorful. It was much more colorful than most of the barns in the Ebensburg area which were all grey. They were so enormous and the houses so little. The fields were buckwheat, whiter than oats or other grains, probably just harvested. The white buckwheat fields throughout that area were always wonderful in their patterns and designs for painting.

Duncan and I had driven out in our car that day. Our chauffeur, John Simuro, was driving. Duncan painted the first picture standing on the road with the canvas in back of the car—a picture of a dramatically curving road leading up to a church. Then we continued on until we came to this great barn on a hill. It was very exciting as we drove up to it. We stopped again and I started this painting. Duncan did another smaller painting of the same scene.

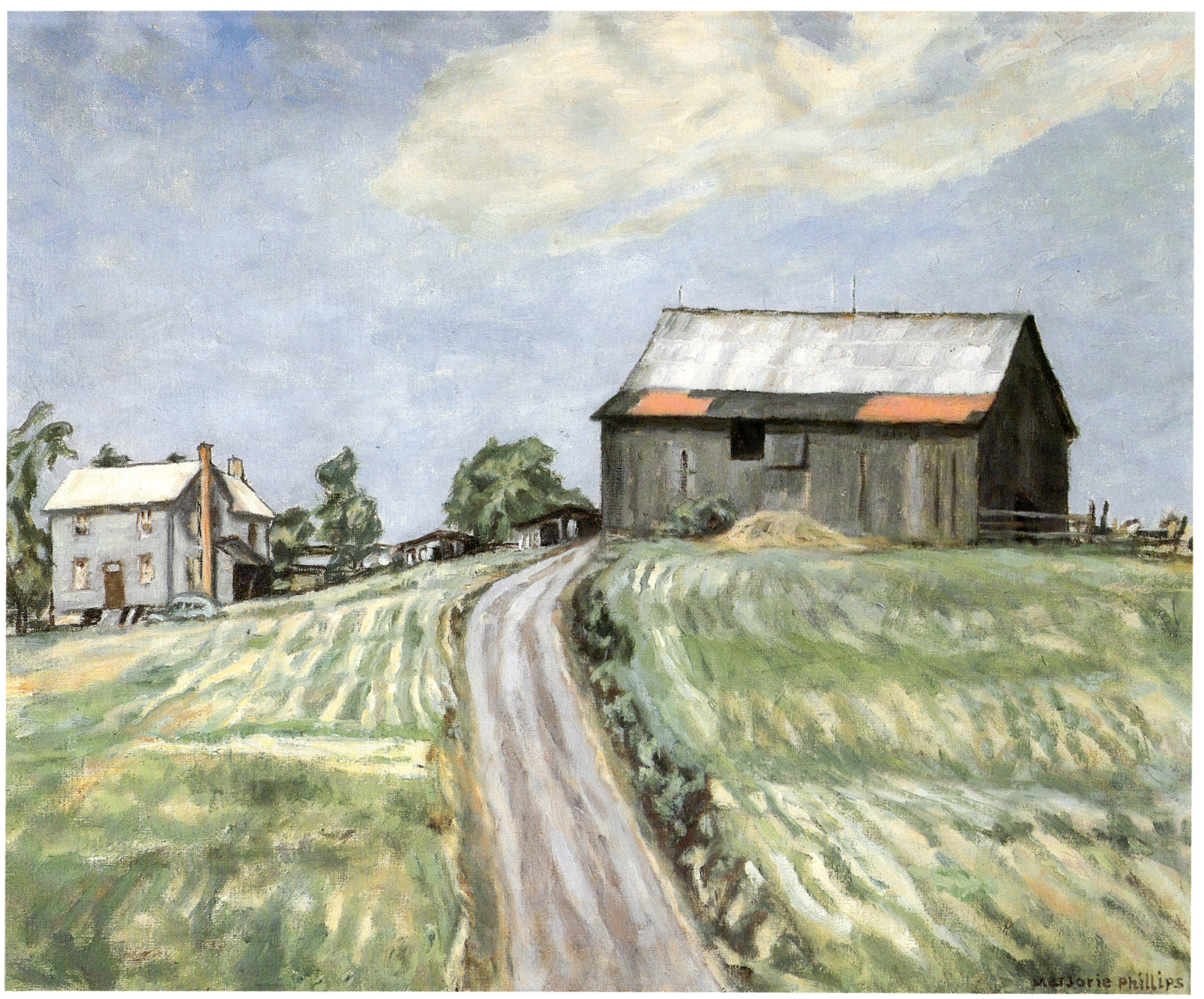
Marjorie Phillips

VIOLETS AND GARDENIA

1946. Oil on canvas, 12 × 9⅞ inches
Laughlin Phillips, Washington, D.C.

1946 was a good period. The war was over, and people had a feeling of relief. The violets and gardenia were given to me by Duncan on some occasion. It could have been my birthday. Duncan gave me flowers all during our married life. He always gave me red roses on occasions like Christmas. The pitcher is rose lustre. He loved lustre, and so did I.

The painting was done in my studio in Washington. I liked the grey background of *Little Bouquet* and wanted to do something like it for another bouquet. The red of the paint in the tube gives a good little touch. A contrast.

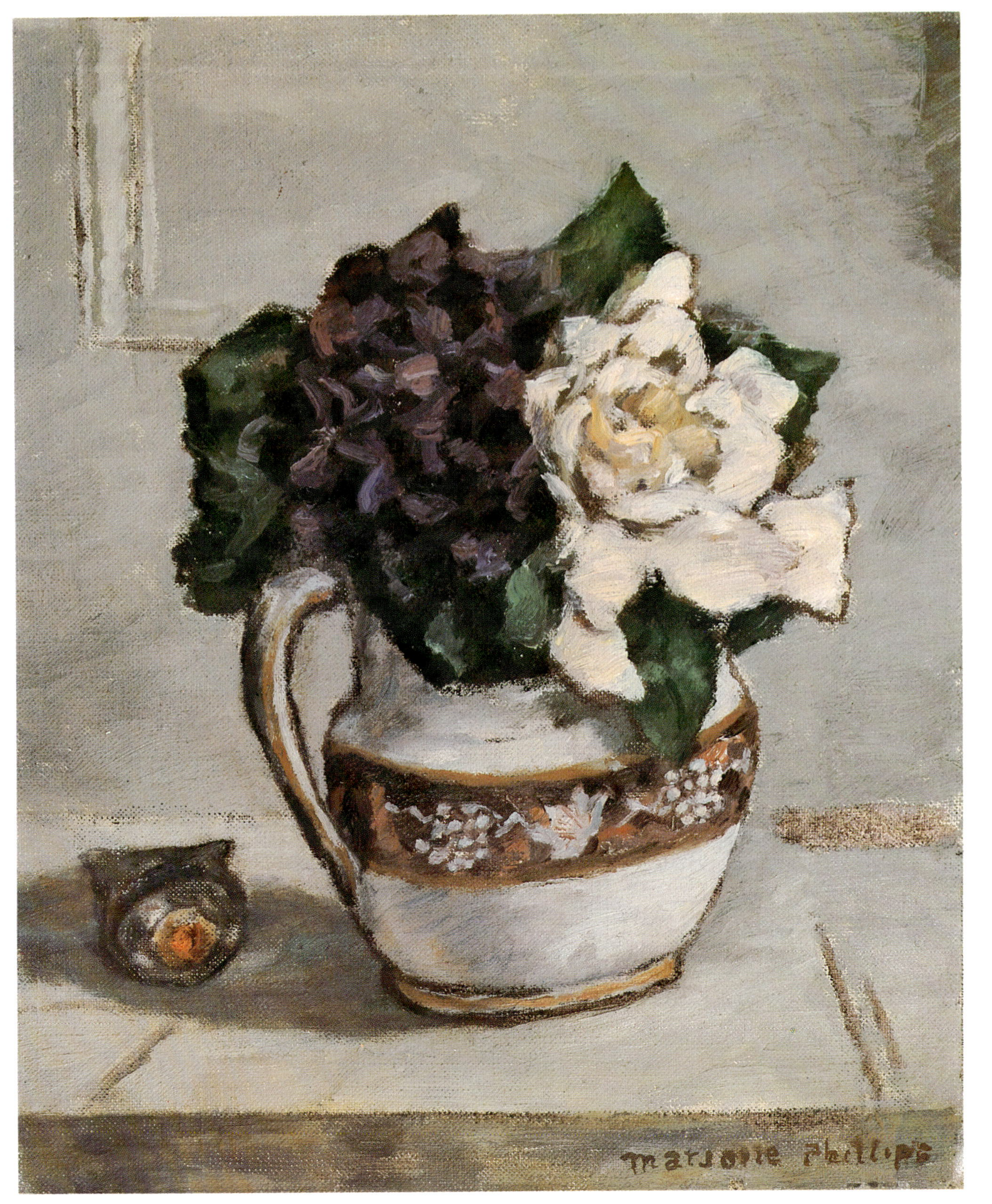
Marjorie Phillips

THE BUZZARD

c. 1947–48. Oil on canvas, 35⅝ × 26 inches
Yale University Art Gallery
Gift of Collection Société Anonyme

This painting was done when you could see the Potomac River from the terrace of our home. The trees have grown up now, and the river is hidden behind them. We had so many buzzards then, it was just natural to put one in. I think of it as a locust tree picture myself.

Duncan and I used to have tea with Katherine Dreier at the Colony Club in New York. We had both taken a liking to Miss Dreier, and knew her as a person who loved art. She had started the Société Anonyme which was quite famous because it was one of the first galleries of modern art in the country. It was very daring, and had started out in the two or three rooms that I had visited as an art student.

Miss Dreier told me that she must have one of my pictures. I was very flattered and agreed to give her one. Marcel Duchamp was her curator at that time, and he came down to Washington to make a selection of an Arthur Dove painting. When he and Duncan went to The Phillips Gallery together, he also picked out *The Buzzard*. Duncan was pleased for me because he knew that I was pleased. Miss Dreier eventually donated part of the Société Anonyme collection to Yale University, where the painting is now.

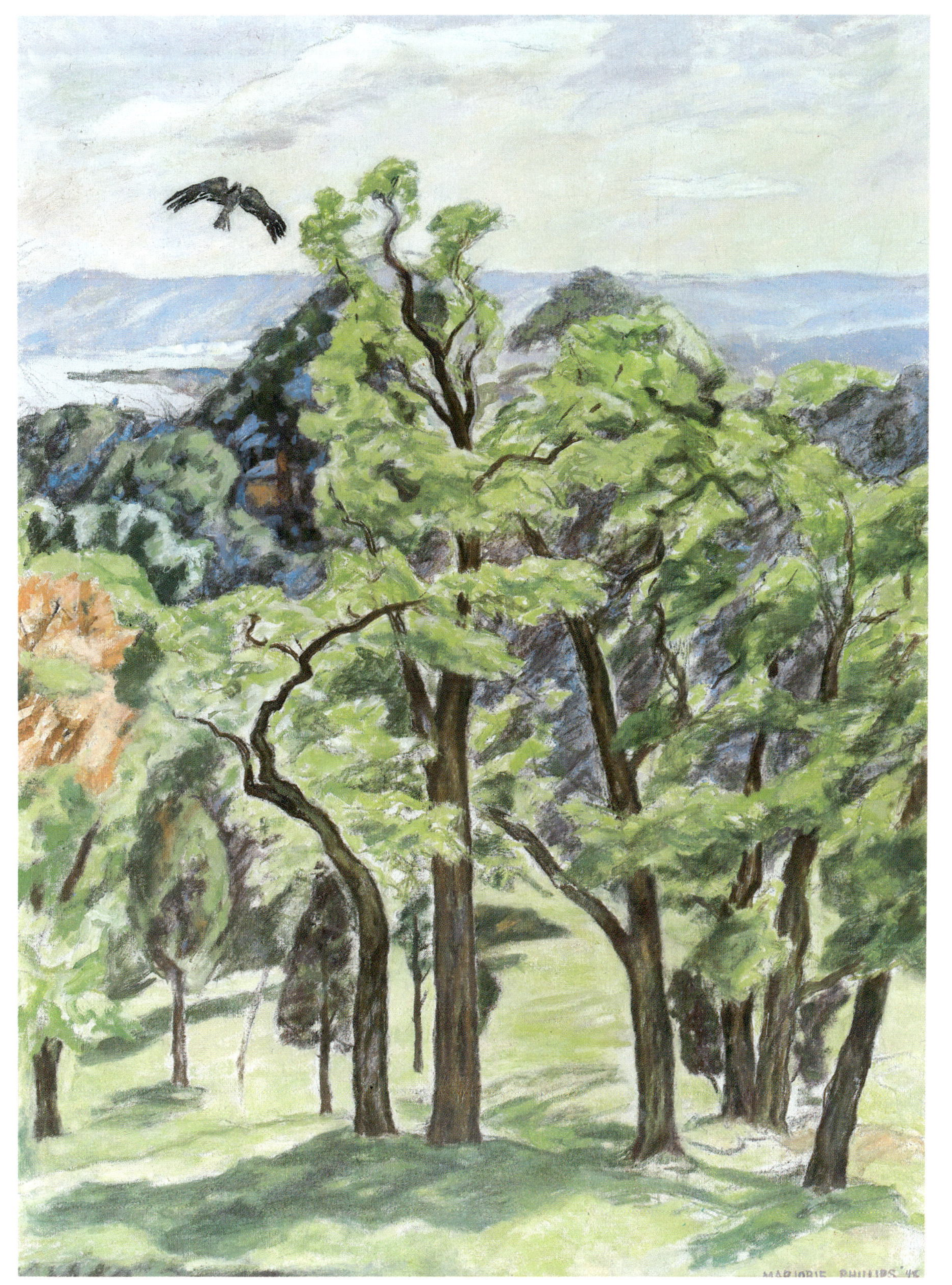
MARJORIE PHILLIPS

ORCHID AND PALETTE

1950. Oil on canvas, 13¾ × 16¼ inches
The Phillips Collection, Washington, D.C.

Perhaps by chance the orchid was standing on the table near my palette. They were such an interesting contrast that I felt they *must* be painted together. My hunch proved to be good and this painting actually turned out to be one of my husband's favorites of my canvases.

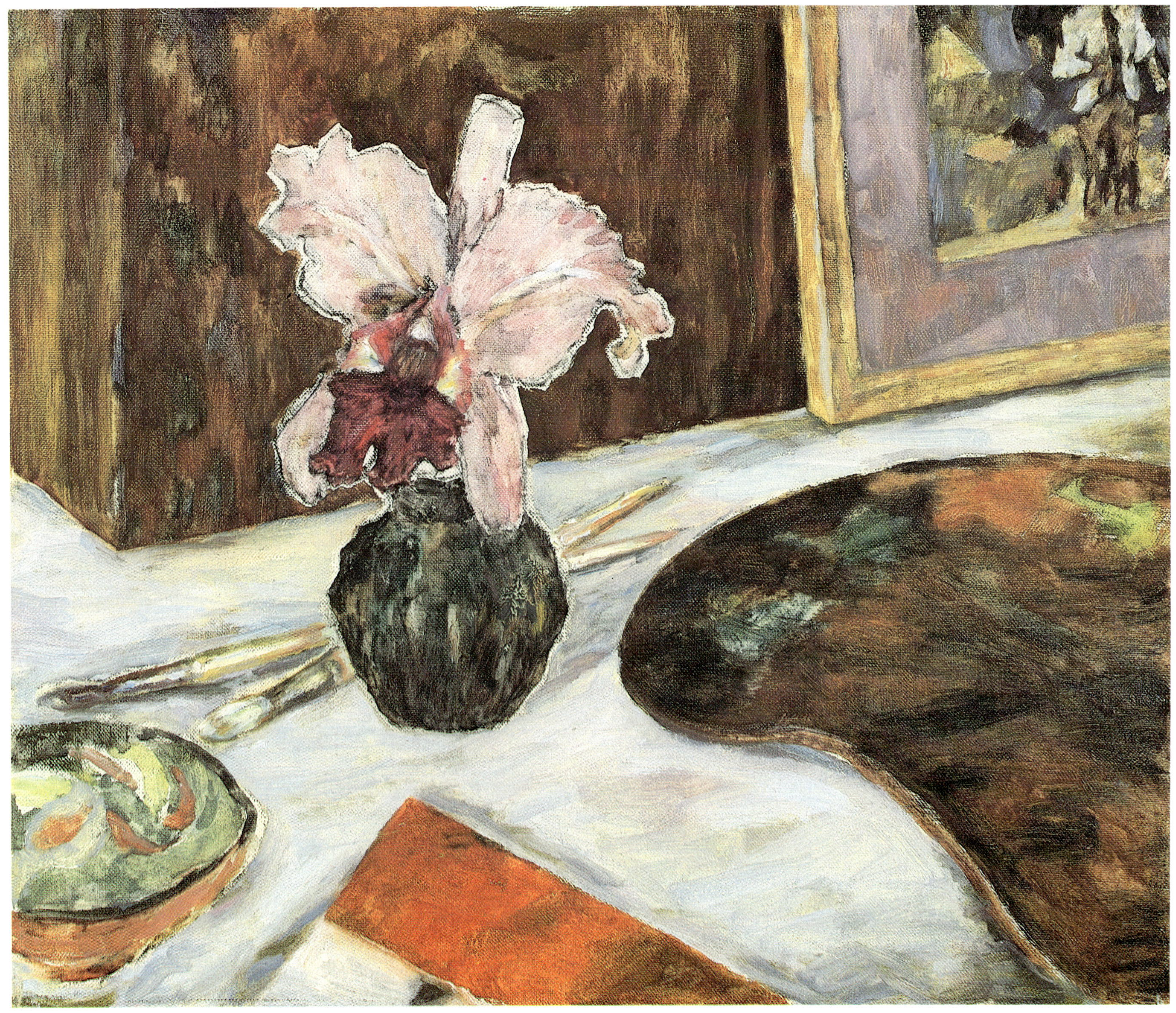

NIGHT BASEBALL

1951. Oil on canvas, 24¼ × × 36 inches
The Phillips Collection, Washington, D.C.

It is a delight for me to write about *Night Baseball* as I had such fun and interest painting it. Of course the central interest is Joe DiMaggio as he waits for the ball about to be pitched. His elegant superanimated stance has great style. I always loved that group of three: the squatting catcher just behind the man at bat and, standing behind him, the eagerly watching umpire leaning forward with responsibility of decision.

Duncan Phillips was a great baseball fan. I always went with him to baseball games and found that I enjoyed them more and more. I had not known the game before we were married. I would always make some pencil drawings of the grandstands, the dugout with players waiting, the plan of the baseball diamond, etc. I noted the color in the seated crowds at Griffith Stadium where the games were held at that time. One year we won the pennant and the city went wild.

This final version of all my studies must have seemed authentic because years later when I loaned this painting for exhibition at the Palace of the Legion of Honor in San Francisco a man from Wildenstein's in New York City wanted to buy it for the Baseball Hall of Fame in Cooperstown, New York. I said I could not sell it as I had given it to my husband.

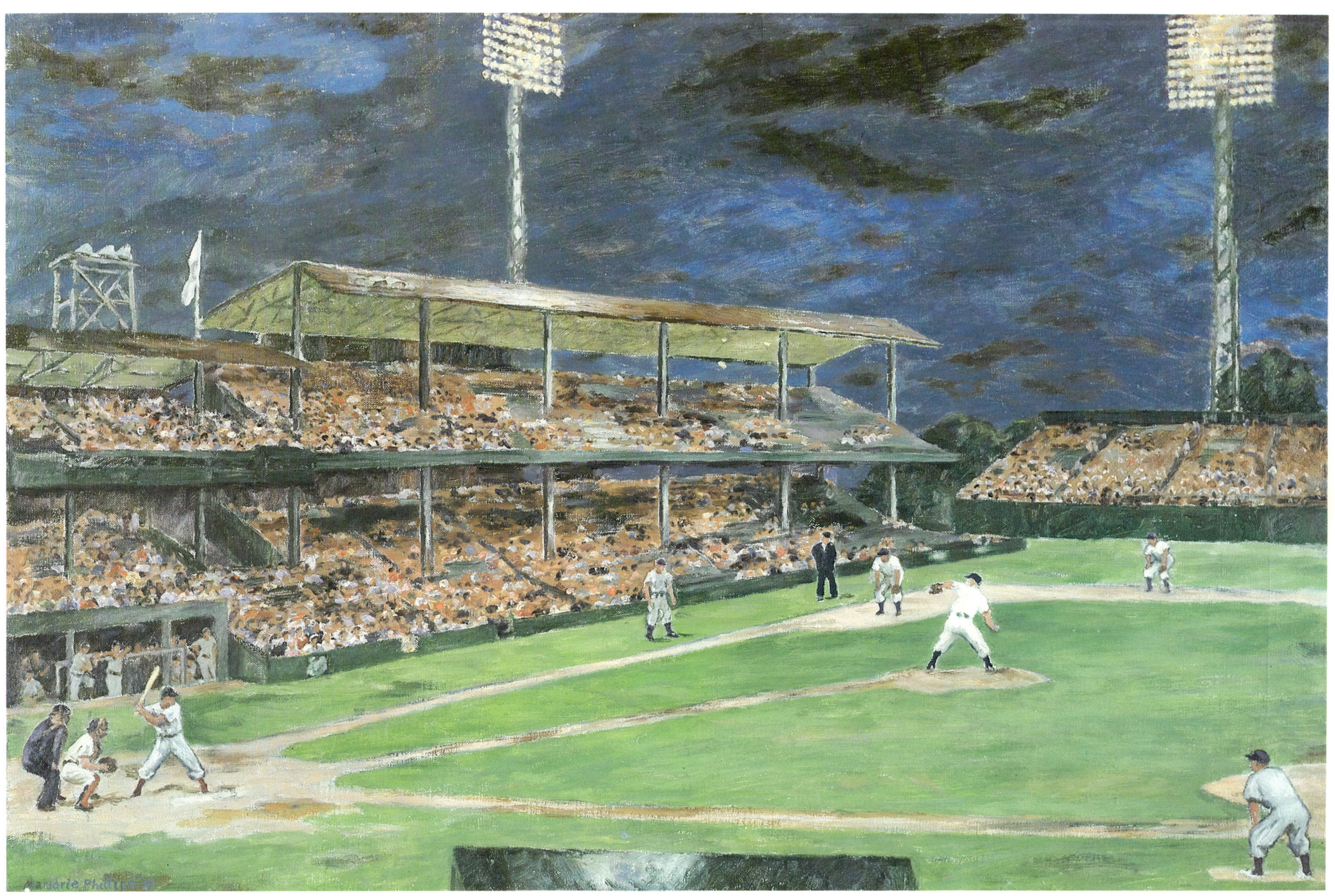

NASTURTIUMS

1951. Oil on canvas, 14⅛ × 11¾ inches
The Phillips Collection, Washington, D.C.

In one of my shows at Durlacher Brothers this little painting could have been sold over and over. But Duncan had been the first to want it and it has been shown a lot in the collection ever since; perfect for narrow walls on either the first or second floor of the museum.

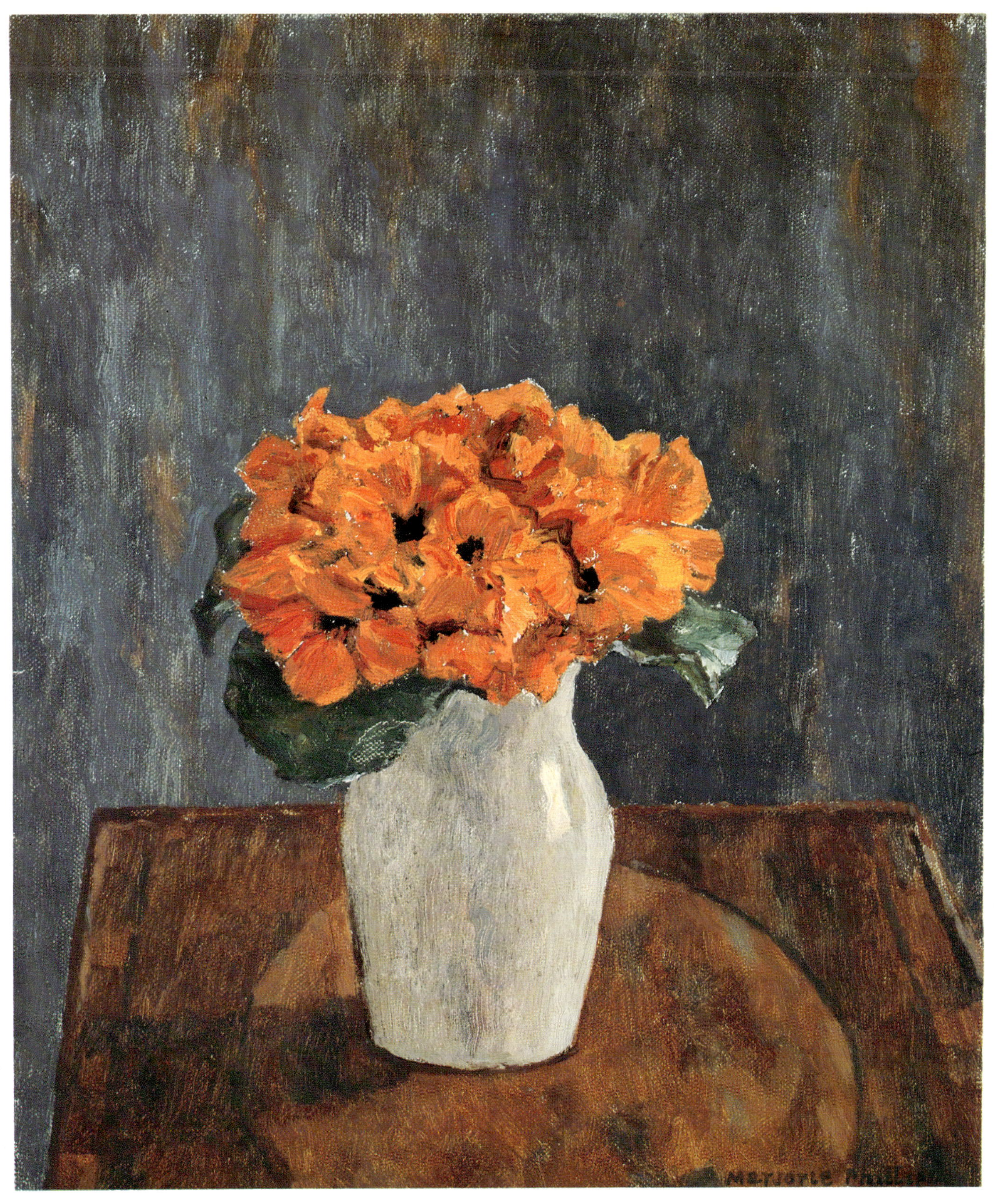
Marjorie

CONVERSATION PIECE

1953. Oil on canvas, 24 × 34 inches
Liza Phillips, Washington, D.C.

This was a summer afternoon in 1953 on the front lawn of our house in Ebensburg. The two posts were the front entrance to the house and led out to the road that Mademoiselle and I were walking on in the painting *Morning Walk*. Mother Phillips had every kind of maple planted on the place. She loved maples. Of course they grew up rather densely.

These were happy times. The figures are Duncan, Laughlin, myself and our three poodles, C'est Tout, Ami, and Babette. Laughlin must have been about 29 and had just returned from Hanoi, where he was stationed in the foreign service. He was visiting from his home in Washington, D.C.

As you know, "conversation piece" is a term that's used for something odd or a little unusual. The painting is unusual because of the dogs in it, and the particular action. Duncan is throwing a ball to C'est Tout, who was a great ball player. Duncan used to play with the dogs quite a bit and would take them walking. I would go, too, into the woods. We had about eleven acres to our property plus thirty acres of woods that were very hilly.

The dogs used to have terrible tussles, but they never really fought. They could have gone into fights I think but C'est Tout always sat down or lay down at just the right moment. He was the peaceful one. He would have been a champion except for a little white spot.

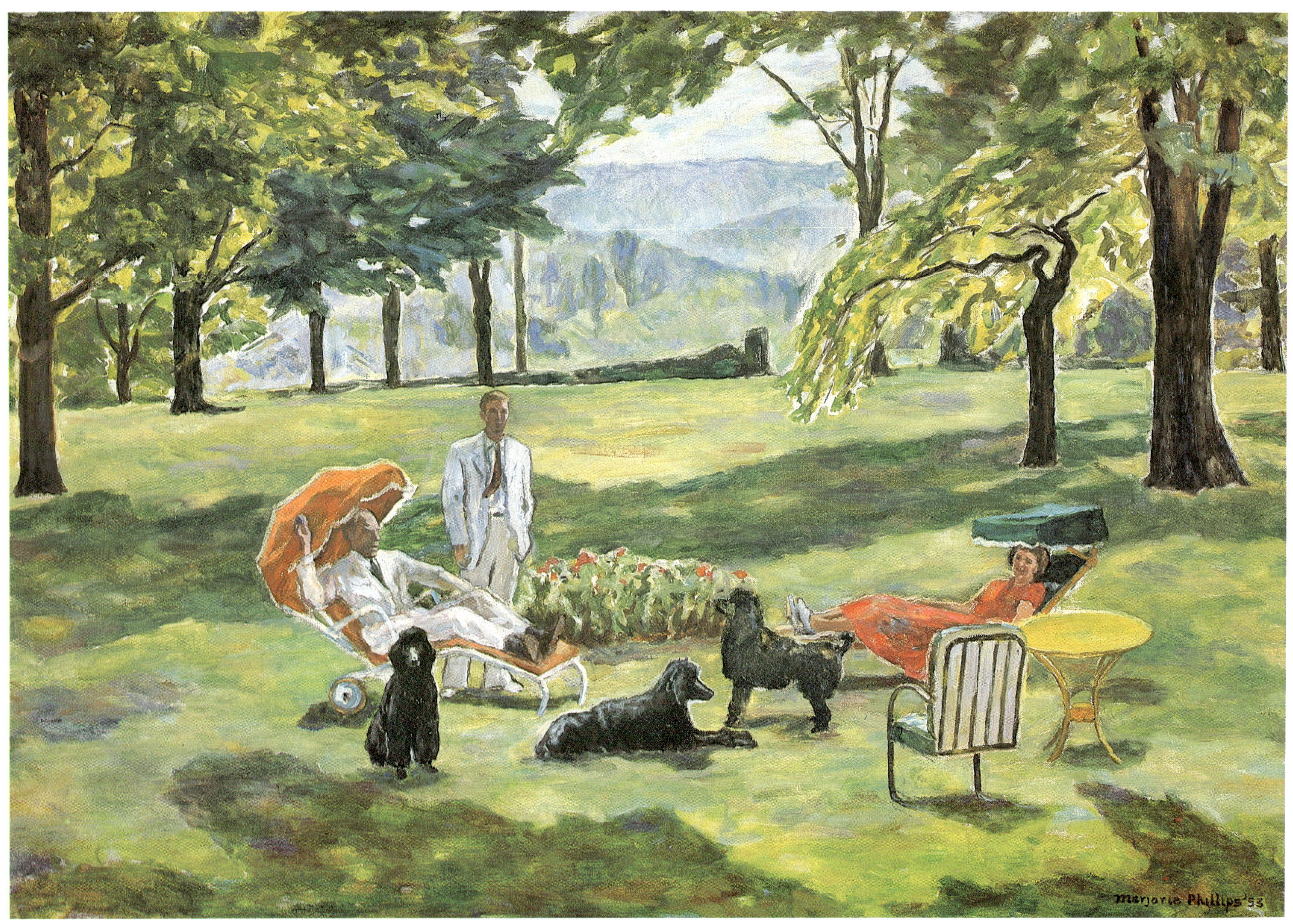
Marjorie Phillips '53

PHILODENDRON

1953 or 1954. Oil on canvas, 40⅛ × 31⅞ inches
The Phillips Collection, Washington, D.C.

I thought that this philodendron plant was magnificent. I wanted to paint it three-dimensionally, bringing out the objects around it with their simple tub or drum shapes—the lamp shades, the pot that the plant stands in, the table top. The reddish tone of the curtains seems good to me and the blue of the chair picks up the blue of the sky beyond.

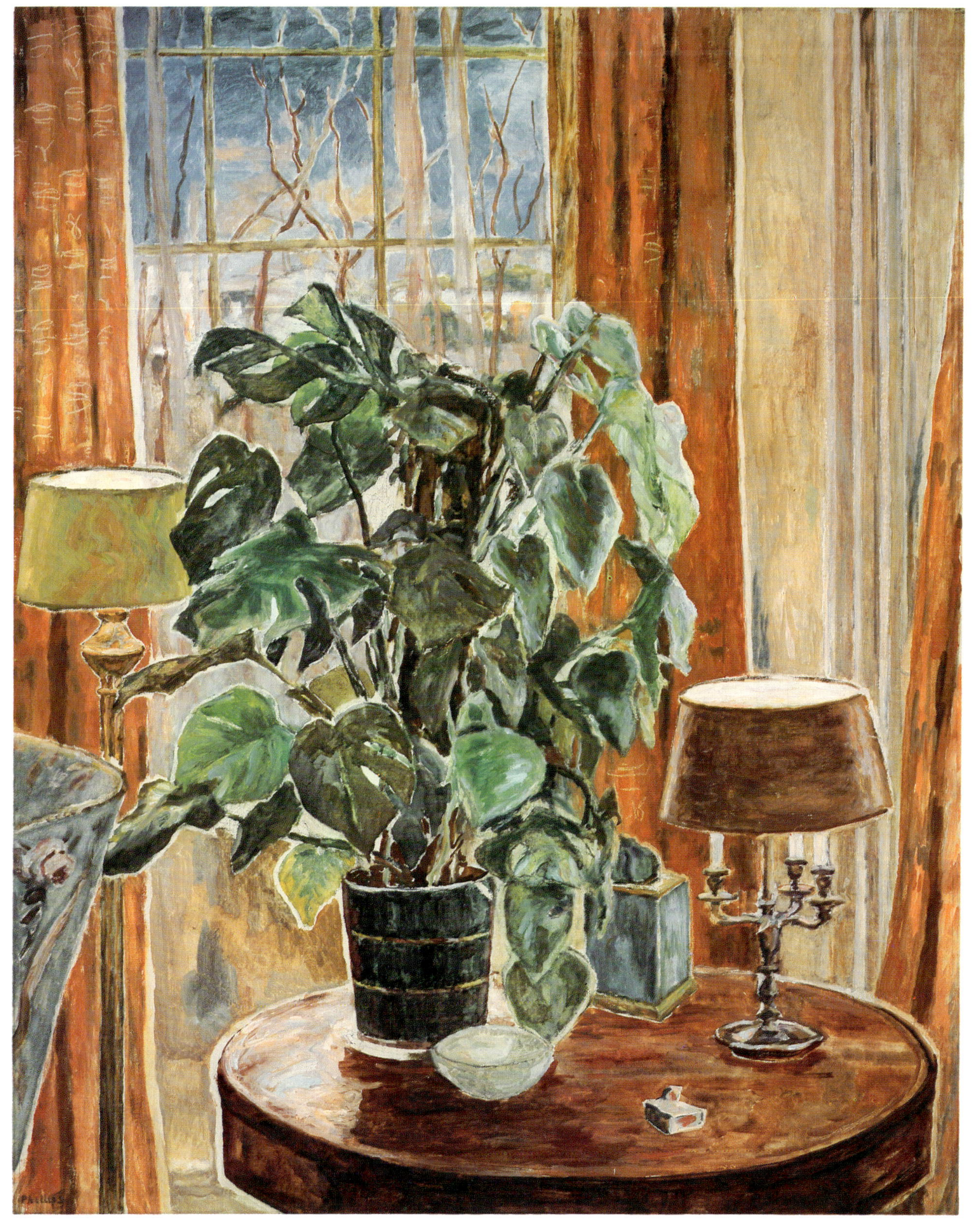

THE BIG PEAR

1955. Oil on canvas, 12⅛ × 14 inches
The Phillips Collection, Washington, D.C.

Paintings are hard to describe. This one I feel is strong in form with a touch of poetry. The strong dissonant note of the back of a book gives me a strange delight. The whites throughout are refreshing and the darks play an equal part; all with great simplification and life.

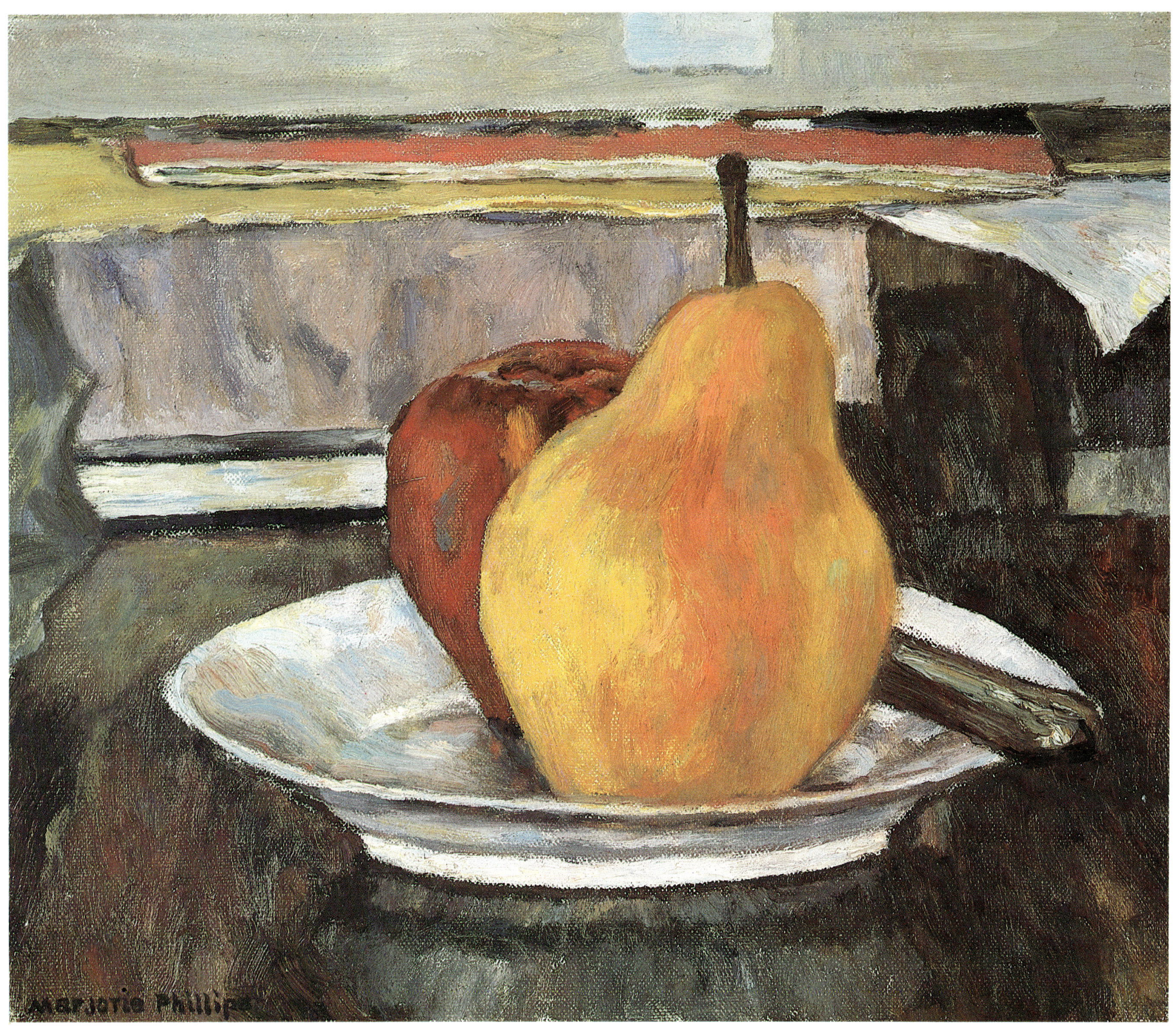
Marjorie Phillips

THE OPEN DOOR

1956. Oil on canvas, sight: 39⅜ × 29¾ inches
The Phillips Collection, Washington, D.C.

Everyone loves an open door, particularly when it opens on a lovely view, and as it turns out this painting from our south entrance showing the view to the distant Potomac River is no exception. When I painted it we could see the river from that level! In the meantime the trees between have grown so high that now one sees that view only from the second floor. Sometimes I think they will reach the sky!

The diagonal shadows thrown are from the columns supporting the porch itself. What an enchanting place to sit and read or draw, converse, and watch the life around, the dogs chasing squirrels, the birds, and all the colors and sounds of a very favorite place!

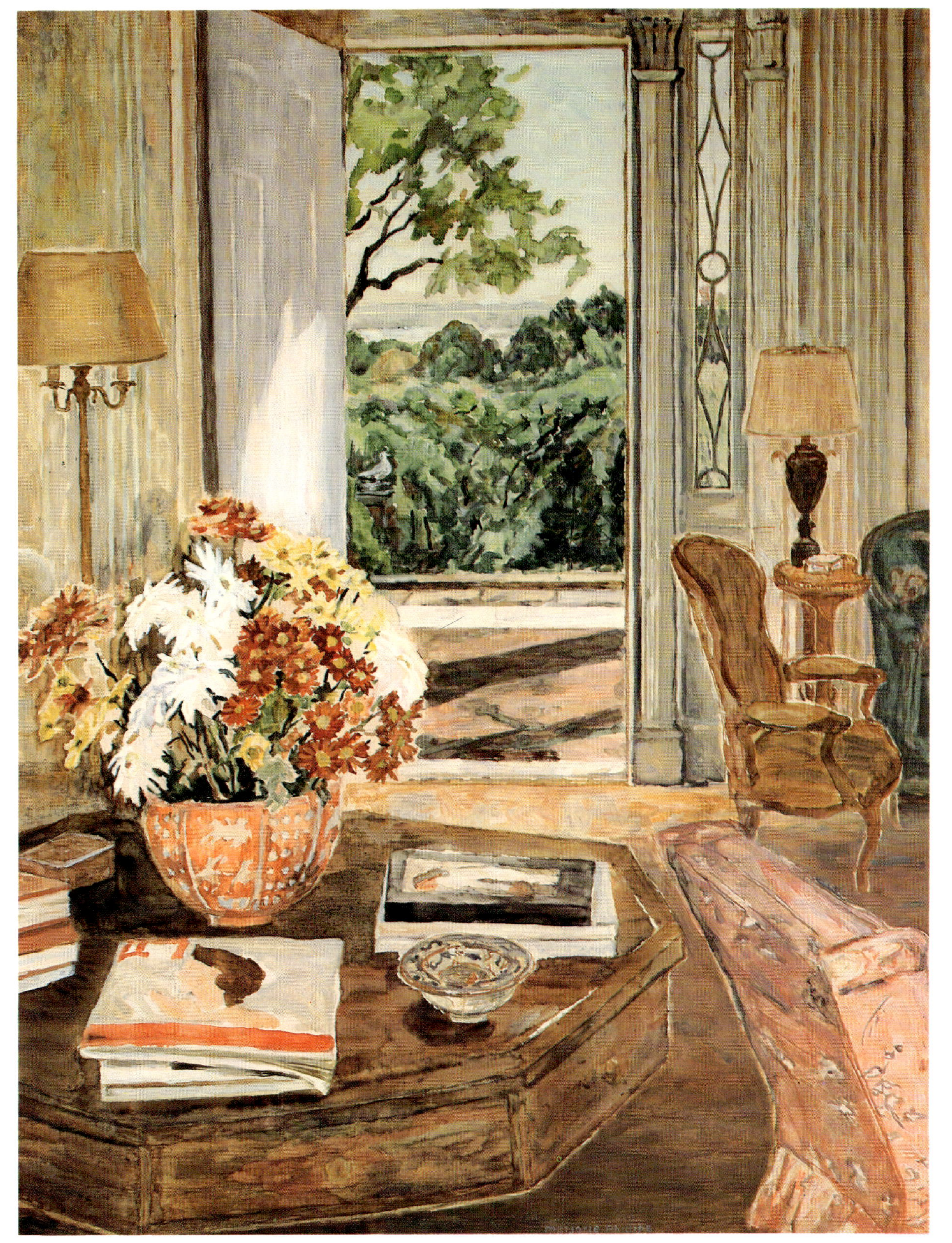

PATH TO THE STUDIO

1957. Oil on canvas, 22 × 32 inches
Sylvia Partridge, Washington, D.C.

I often lingered on the path to my studio in Ebensburg, enjoying the long border beds of flowers, the trees, the shadows they cast, the woods, the Owens farm, and the hills beyond. The everchanging sky and cloud patterns were wonderful.

The blue of the sky when I did this painting reminded me of that in a painting in the National Gallery in London, a small Piero della Francesca *Virgin and Child* with an ineffable sky. For all my efforts I could not approach that color. I thought it would have been perfect in this painting!

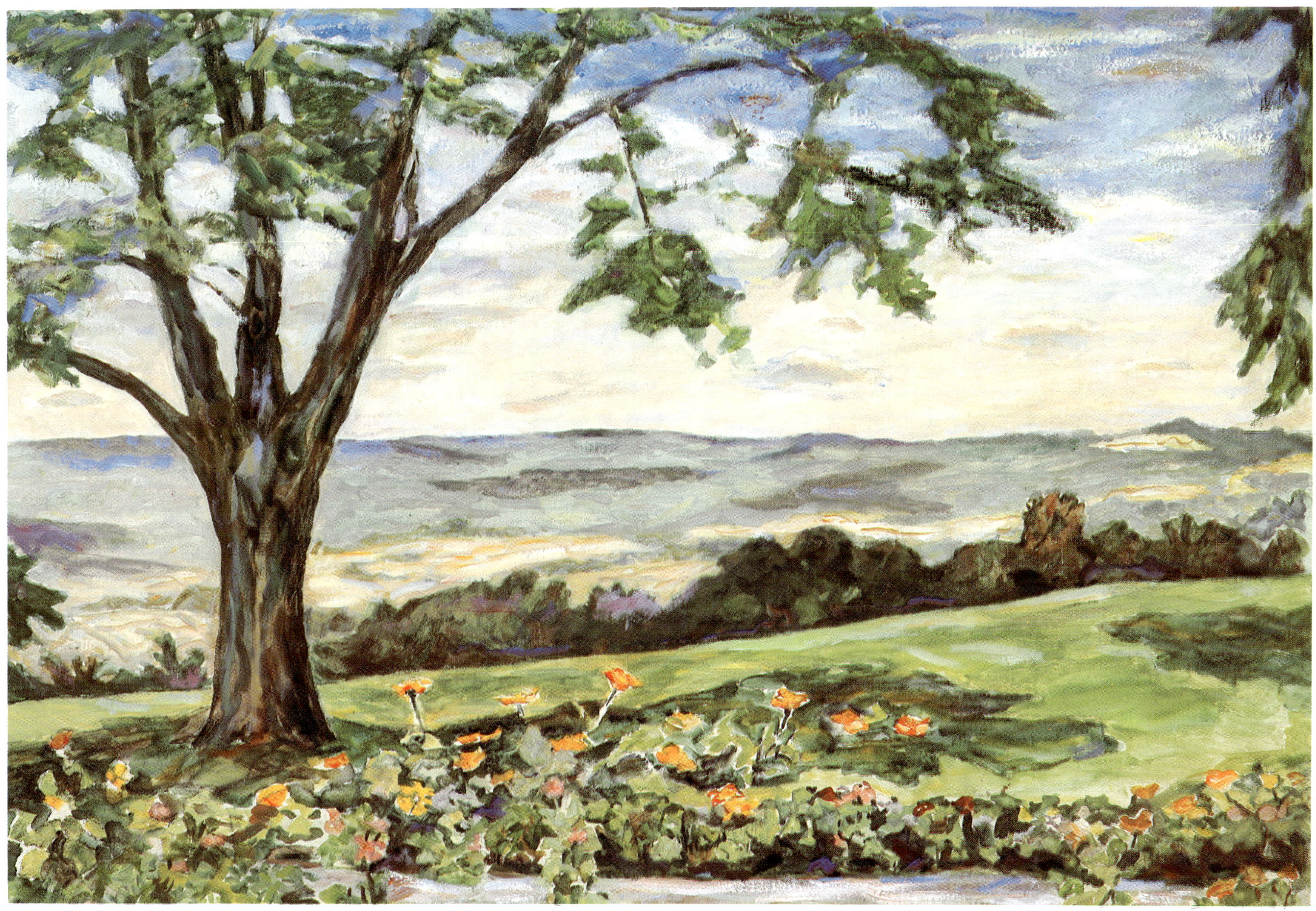

TORCH FLOWERS AGAINST CORAL

1957. Oil on canvas, 34¼ × 24 inches
Smith College, Northampton, Mass.

The torch flowers (Torch Tinctanium) grew in the old fashioned flower beds at the Ebensburg home. They always intrigued and delighted me and I often picked some for still life paintings.

At the time I did this painting I was working in the spacious guest bathroom on the second floor of the house where there was a large window with perfect north light. Some coral tiles there inspired me to use that color for the background.

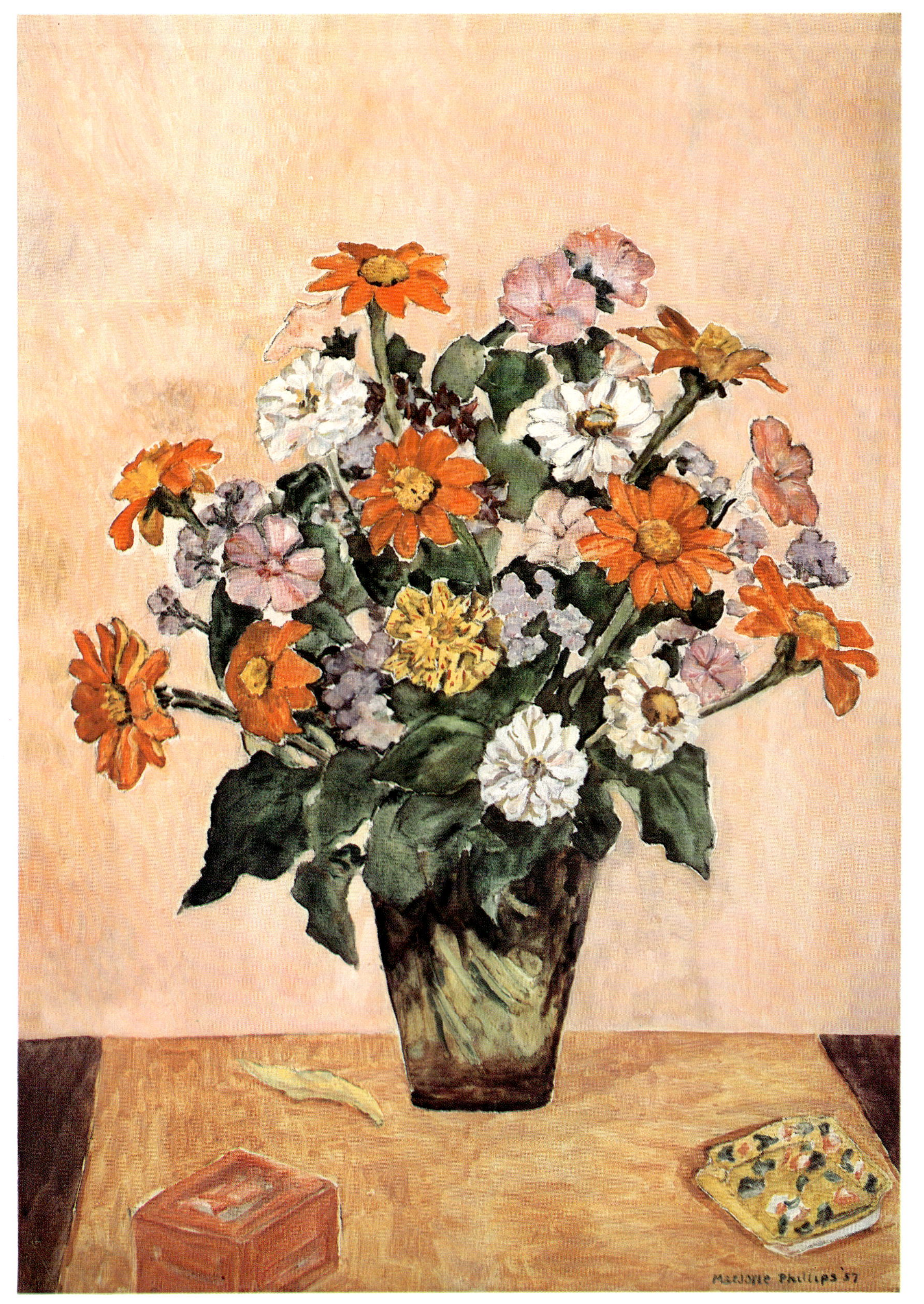
Marjorie Phillips '57

NECTARINES AND BOTTLE OF WINE

1959. Oil on canvas, 22 × 28 inches
California Palace of the Legion of Honor, San Francisco, California

I am always pleased to remember that Betty Parsons, the connoisseur dealer, picked this painting, *Nectarines and Bottle of Wine*, as her *favorite* in one of my exhibitions at Durlachers.

It was painted in my perfect bathroom studio in the house at Ebensburg, the background reflecting the coral tiles!

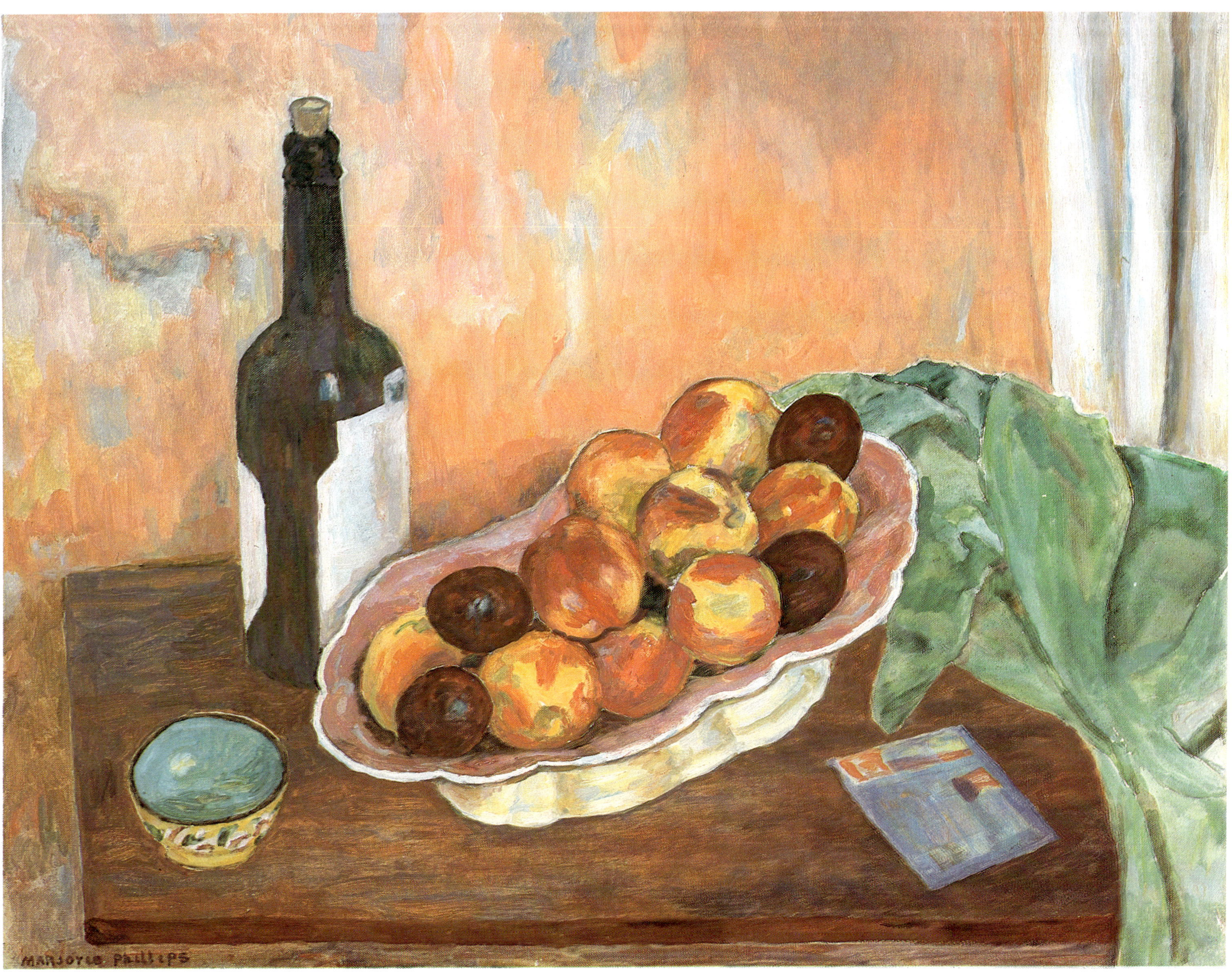
MARJORIE PHILLIPS

TOWN AND MOUNTAINS

1959. Oil on canvas, 32 × 39⅞ inches
The Phillips Collection, Washington, D.C.

I feel that *Town and Mountains* is really exciting in subject, composition, and color. It was done from the southeastern corner of our place at Ebensburg, beyond the tennis court. The road with traffic is the main highway to Pittsburgh. The red building was the only factory at that time, and was built on the edge of town.

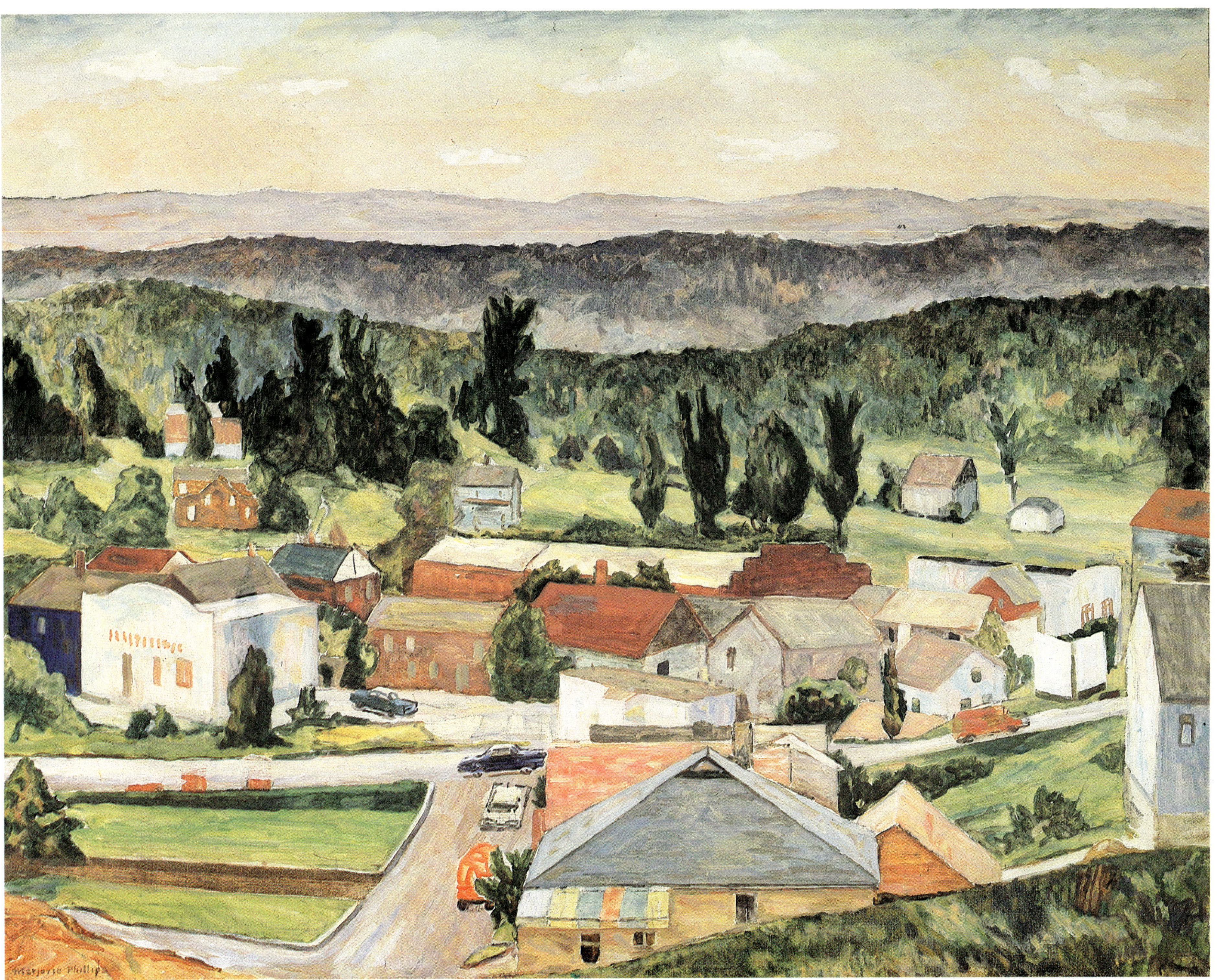
Marjorie Phillips

LAUGHLIN AND BABY DUNCAN
1960. Oil on canvas, 12 × 17 inches
Laughlin Phillips, Washington, D.C.

This is a painting of my son, Laughlin, and his son, Duncan, who was then about six months old. Laughlin and his wife, Betty, had just returned from a tour of duty with the foreign service in Tehran, and baby Duncan was born here in Washington. I was a happy grandmother, and did the sketch for this painting in the living room of my house. I threw the original sketch up on a screen and did the painting from that.

Baby Duncan was very intense and alert. I had a tea party for him when he was about five. It was on Lincoln's birthday and we had a toy rocket which we sent up. I was thinking how charming he was and I was telling him all the wonderful things about Lincoln, how big he was, how kind and wise, how he had humor. Duncan looked at me and said "Are you Lincoln?" Isn't that charming? I'll never forget it. I must have meant those things to him. It shows his mind working, putting two and two together. He was a very lovable child.

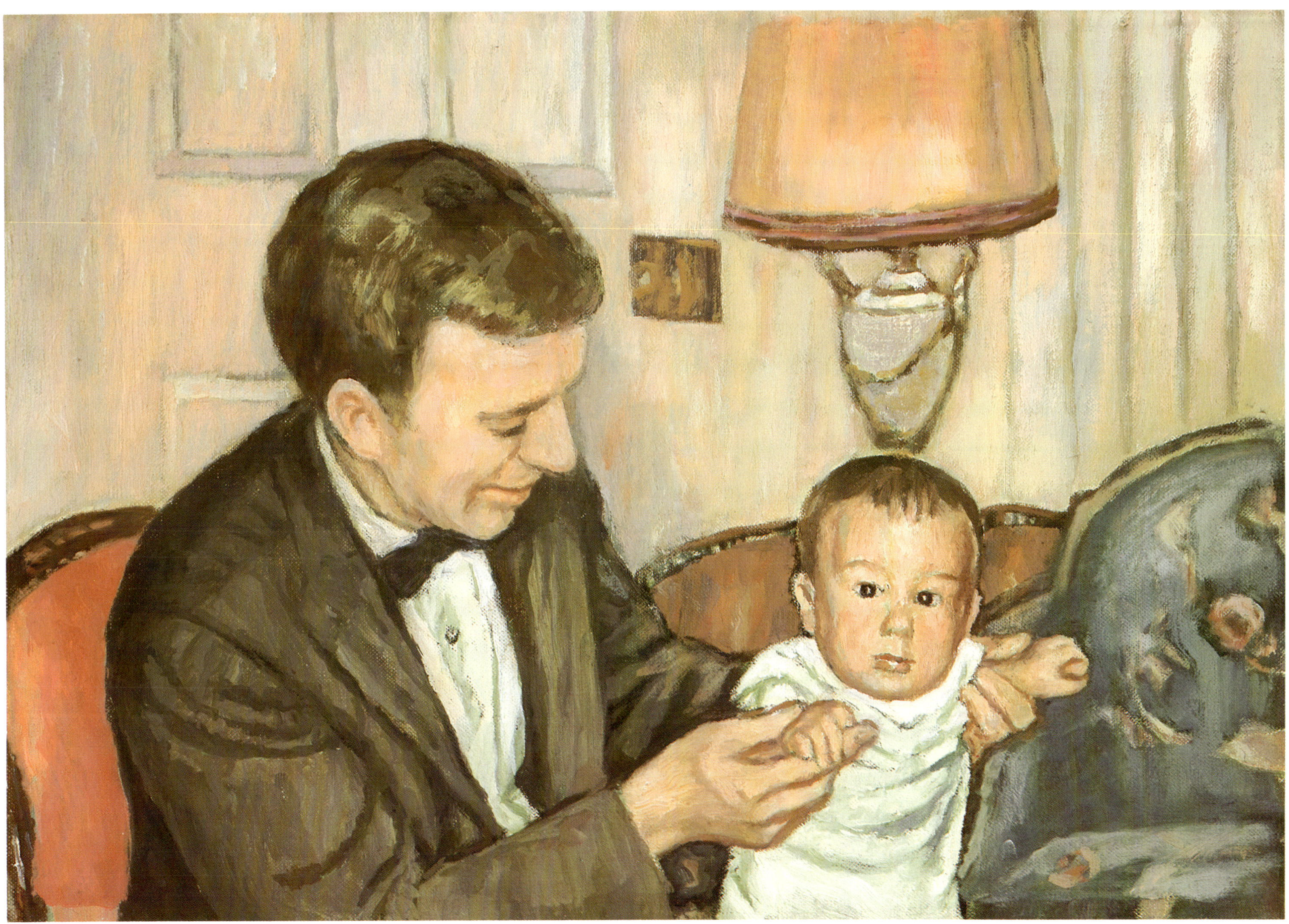

EARLIEST TULIPS

1975. Oil on canvas, 20 × 18 inches
Matthew Huxley, Chevy Chase, Md.

These tulips came from the florist over at Johnson's Flower Center. I wanted to bring them home and paint them because they were the first tulips of the season. The African violets at the bottom give a piquant little contrast. There's a heavy use of paint in some areas and a much lighter use in other areas that's typical of many of my paintings.

My dear friend Judith Huxley was here for lunch one day. She said that she didn't have a painting of mine and that she'd like one. I said that I'd love to give her one. I got out several. This one wasn't even mounted—it was just dangling over my arm. She spotted it immediately and said that it was the one she loved, so I mounted it up and gave it to her. Her husband, Matthew Huxley, took such an interest in hanging it. I was very touched. After long contemplation, he hung it in the living room of their home over a small Chinese bronze statue of a lion. It was stunning. He really made an artistic wall.

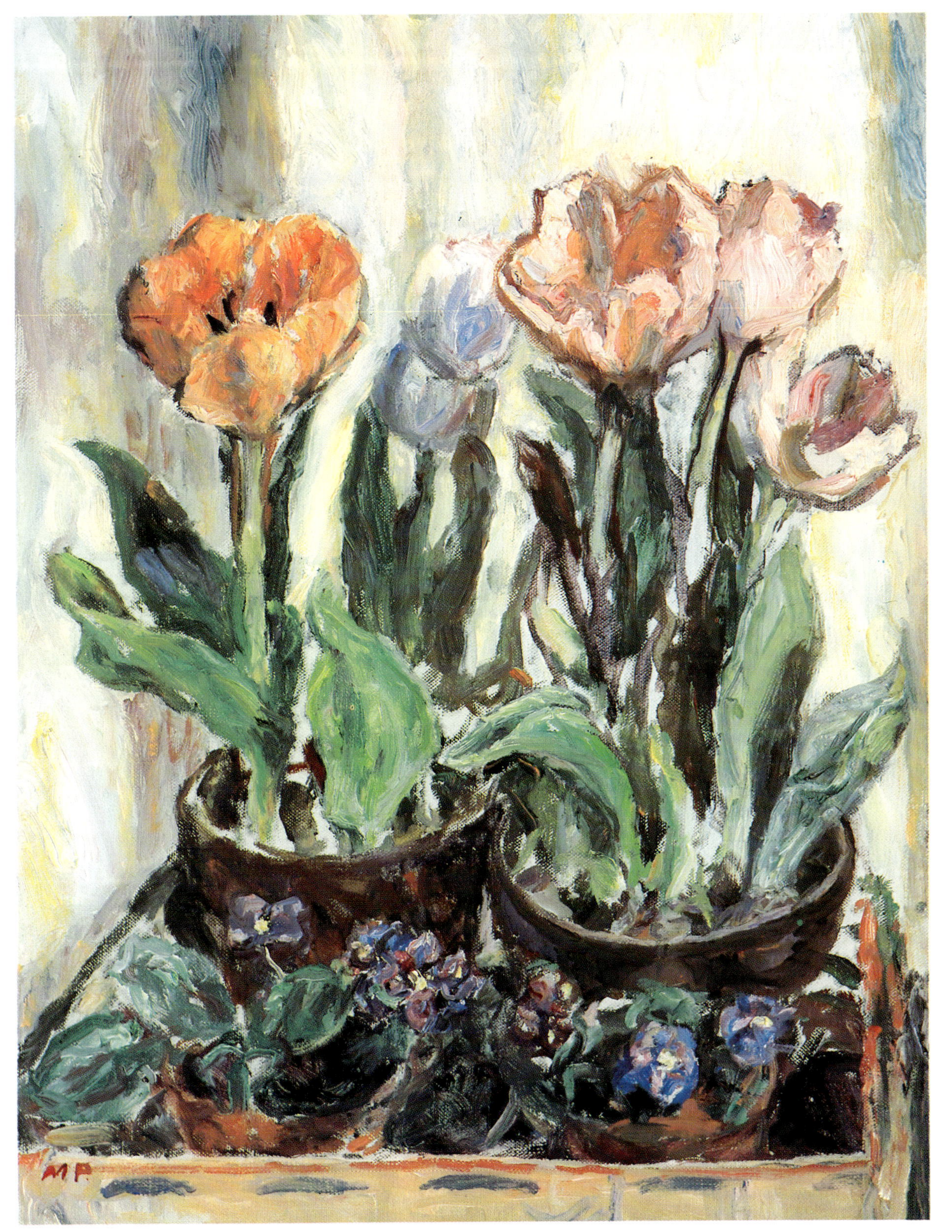
MP

PORTRAIT OF DUNCAN

1975. Oil on canvas, 40 × 32 inches
The Phillips Collection, Washington, D.C.

I wanted to do a portrait of Duncan just for myself as an overmantel in the studio. I did not feel that any of the other portraits emphasized the distinguished and beautifully sensitive character of the head and brow of the man I loved. This portrait was done in about 1975 after I retired as director of The Phillips Collection in 1972 and Laughlin took over. It was quite a few years after Duncan's death in 1966.

This pose is a characteristic one. Duncan would often sit in his favorite chair in the living room and read the newspaper. He was vitally interested in politics and world affairs, and would usually read the Washington *Post* and the Washington *Star*. One of his closest friends was Walter Lippmann, the political analyst. The two of them enjoyed many lively discussions during their times together.

We were crazy about our three poodles who all lived for seventeen years. I tried to give each dog its special character. Babette was Duncan's favorite and I wanted to make her a little humorous. Babette used to go out of her head when she saw sky writing. She knew that sky writing was WRONG, and she would try and stop it. She barked and barked and barked until it finally disappeared. What a character! The dog on the left is C'est Tout, the ball catcher in *Conversation Piece*. Ami is just to the right with a long distinguished nose. Ami was my special favorite.

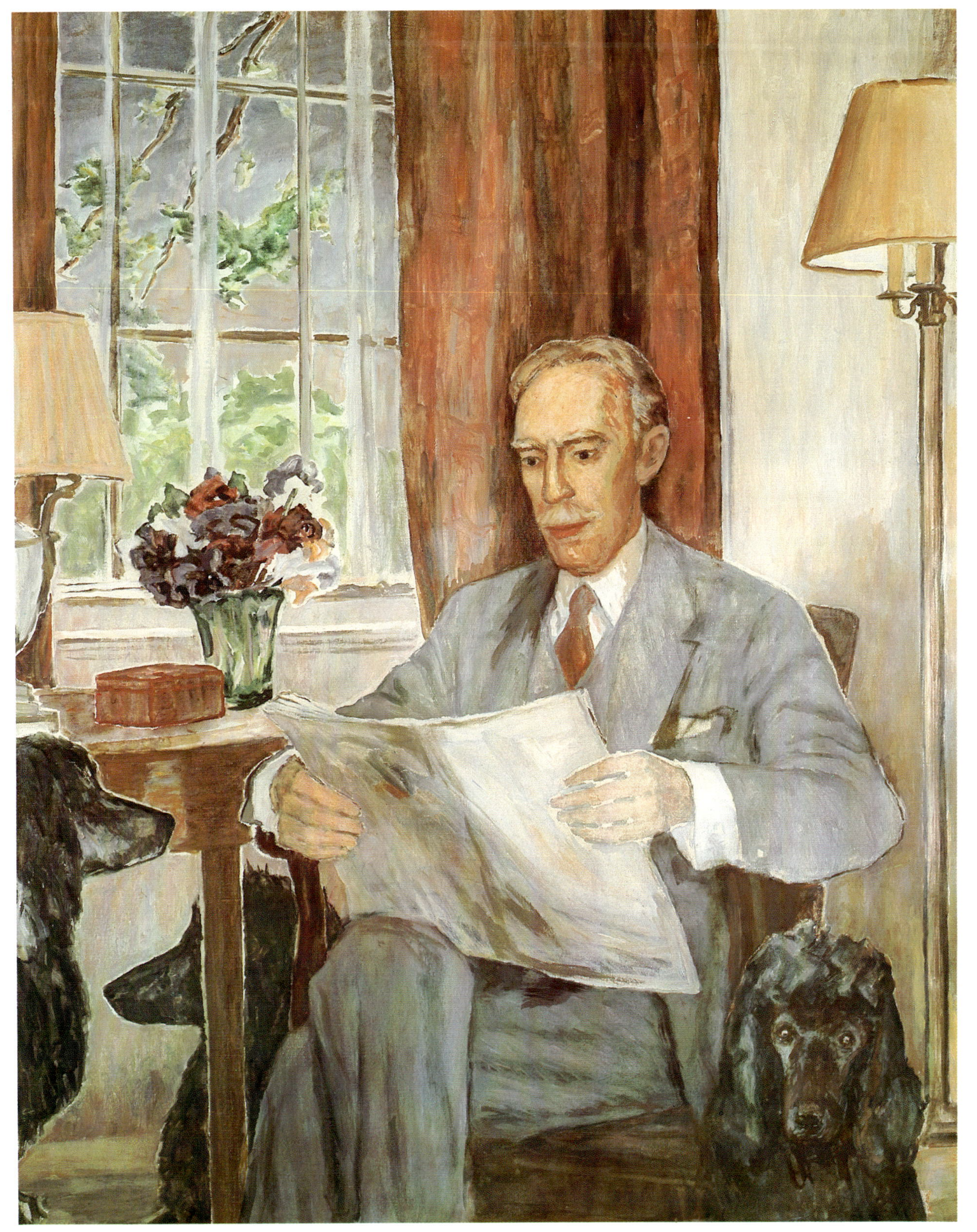

MIXED BOUQUET
1977. Oil on canvas, 20 × 18 inches
Mrs. Henry Mitchell, Washington, D.C.

One day when Virginia Mitchell came for afternoon coffee she brought this bouquet which stars a gorgeous lily. Her husband, Henry Mitchell, grows a garden from which all sorts of surprises come forth. It is a joy to themselves as well as their friends. One can read delightful reports of the progress of the Mitchell garden in his Washington *Post* column, "Earthman."

I put these particular flowers on a little table in my studio which was covered by a woven doily with an orange tone, believing it would be a piquant combination. The painting completed, I gave it to Ginny and she honors it over their living room mantel.

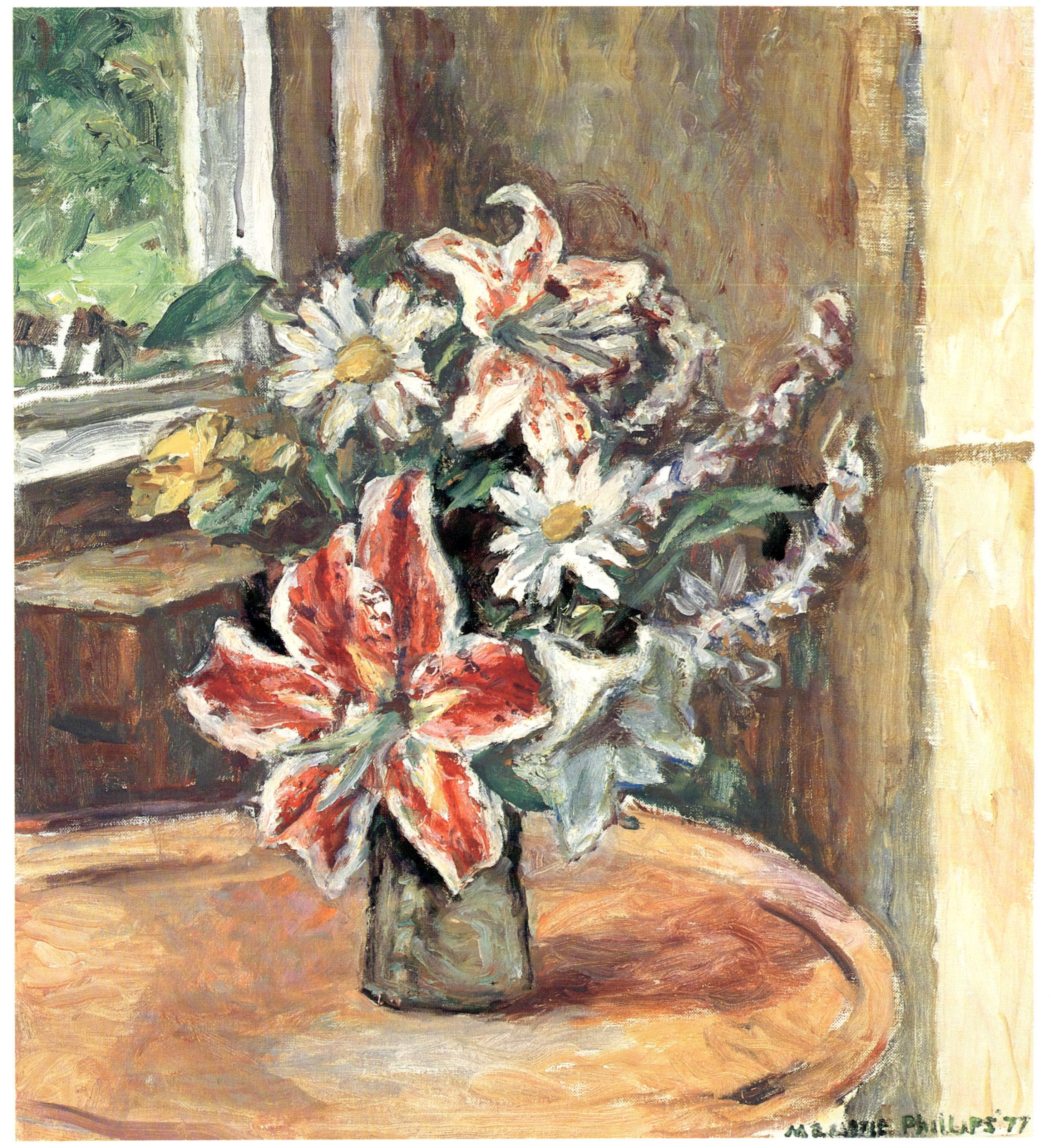
PHILLIPS '77

SELF PORTRAIT
1976–77. Oil on canvas, 23 × 17⅜ inches
The Phillips Collection, Washington, D.C.

I wanted to continue to do portraits and as I was the nearest available model at that time I planned to do a self-portrait. I used the mirror in my Washington, D.C., studio which I normally use to make sure the picture is in balance.

People say this portrait shows both a happy and melancholy side simultaneously. This reminds me of what Pierre Bonnard wrote in one of his notebooks, "When I am happy, I become immediately melancholy."

While working on this I enjoyed the rust color of the jacket I was wearing and had great pleasure in painting the white blouse in contrast.

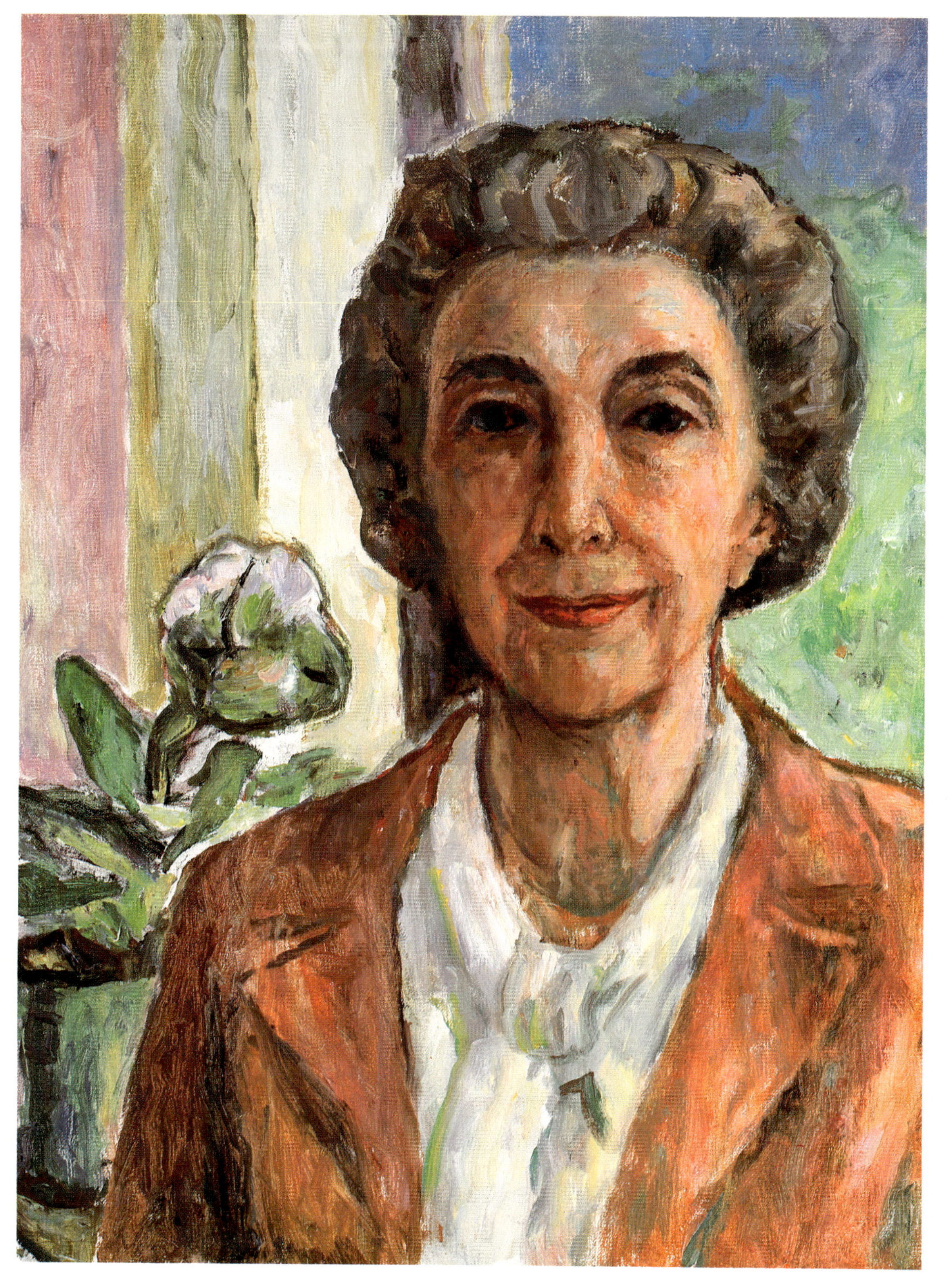

ROSES IN A LALIQUE BOWL

1977. Oil on canvas, 26 × 28 inches

The Phillips Collection, Washington, D.C.

In the early twenties, Lord and Taylor in New York carried distinguished modern objects for sale. Duncan and I happened to find this lovely orange lalique bowl and it has been on the center table of our living room ever since, giving pleasure with its various arrangements of flowers.

In this painting the white blossoms of course are phlox and help to keep the color clear!

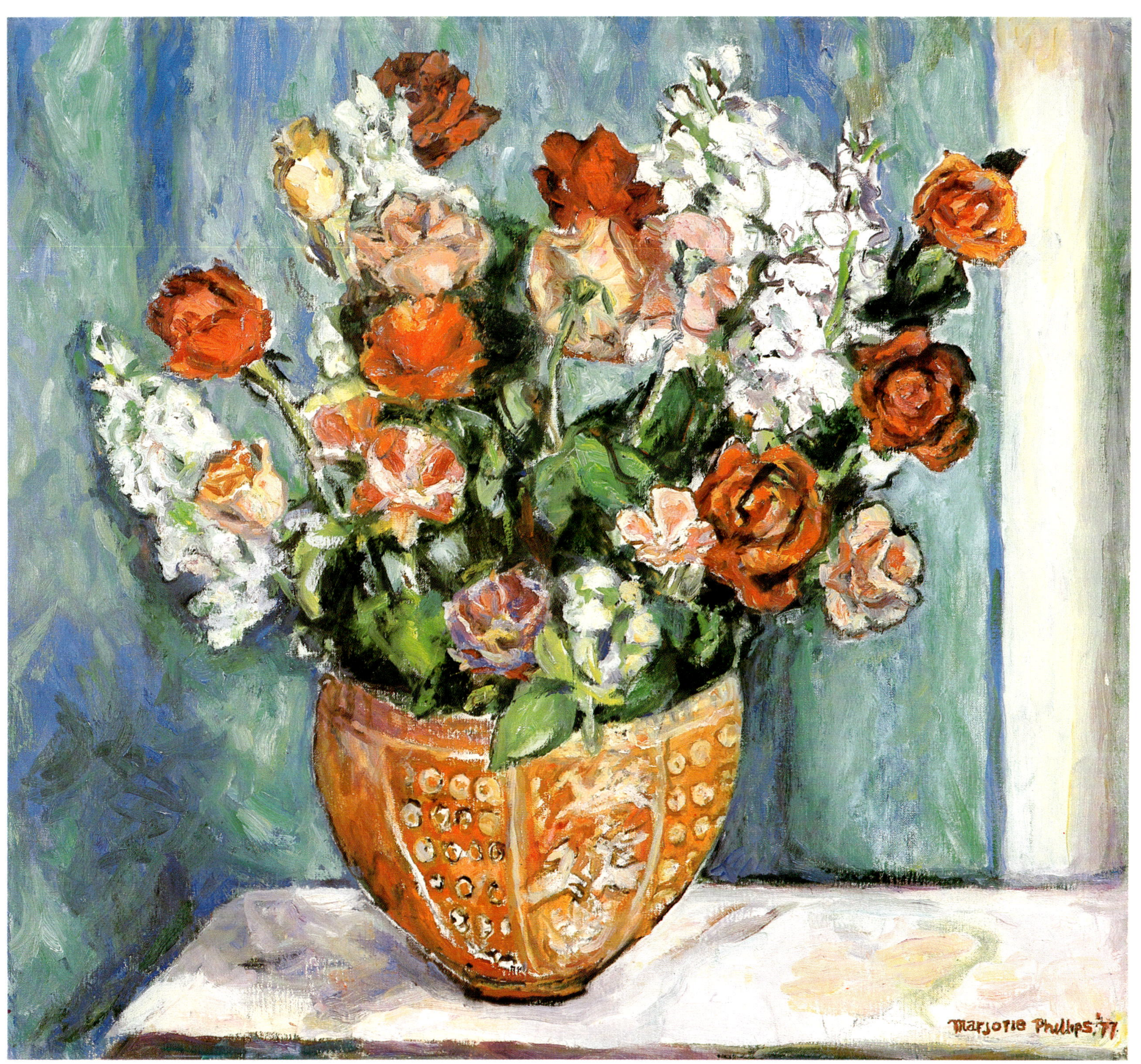
Marjorie Phillips,'77

NOTES AND DRAWINGS

From the time I was about fifteen, I got the habit of promptly writing down thoughts on art on the nearest scrap of paper. You have to catch them when they come to you. This section contains a sampling of these notes, along with some sketches from my notebooks, which are really another form of note taking. Of course, the notes and the sketches don't necessarily relate to each other and they are not in chronological order. Finally, I have included excerpts from recent conversations with my niece, Sylvia Partridge.

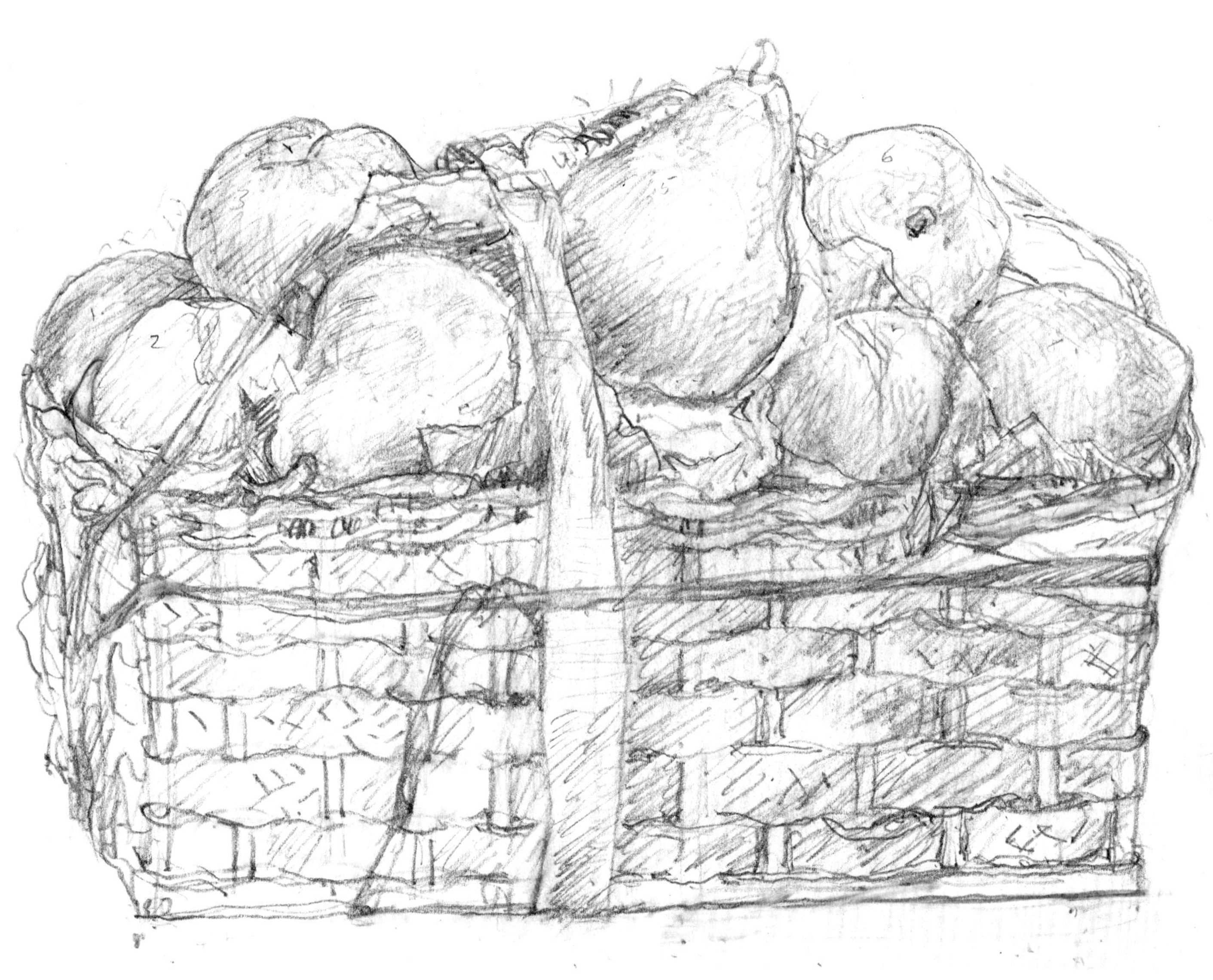

There's an artistic elegance that's different from regular elegance, and it's very important if you can get it. I used to try for that. It gives the essence of the thing, but with taste, and has to do with style. It was always in Watteau's paintings and in most distinguished works.

Bonnard

The great joy and revelation was when we discovered Bonnard. I knew immediately that he was a great colorist. He was so modest and yet so sure of himself. At the end of his life he said that he felt he was just beginning, and I felt that so often of my own work.

I love the strength and subtlety of his painting. The combination is striking. The color relations are so unusual and so human at the same time: of course his color sense is instinctive as well as the result of deep study. He said that he learned the most from Monet. His paintings give me so much satisfaction because I always loved color so. But I was never as daring as Bonnard. He had such vast knowledge and artistic integrity and practised continuous constant observation. For me of course it was one of the main events of a lifetime to meet him because he was a unique personality. You felt the pure artist there.

Duncan and I bought 22 of his paintings. At the present time 16 are in The Phillips Collection and 4 are in my personal collection.

Watteau

Watteau was a beautiful draftsman, a great draftsman, and his work lives forever. He didn't feel that he had to express anything disagreeable. I looked at a great deal of his work when I was about 18 and 19—we had wonderful books at the Art Students League and in our library at home in Ossining. He was an example for me. Some of his work has very substantial realism and solidity, like the one of the cook; and then there were gala parties. The workmanship was always equally wonderful.

Giotto and Piero della Francesca

My favorite murals in Italy were those in the Arena Chapel by Giotto, part of which contain *The Kiss of Judas*, the moving figure of Christ being kissed by Judas at the moment of the betrayal. And my next favorite was "The Story of the True Cross" by Piero della Francesca in the church of S. Francesco in Arrezo. The people, the figures, are all so beautiful and rather impersonal. There's nothing sentimental about them, but a great deal of dignity and warmth. It's worth a trip to Italy. I feel privileged to have seen them.

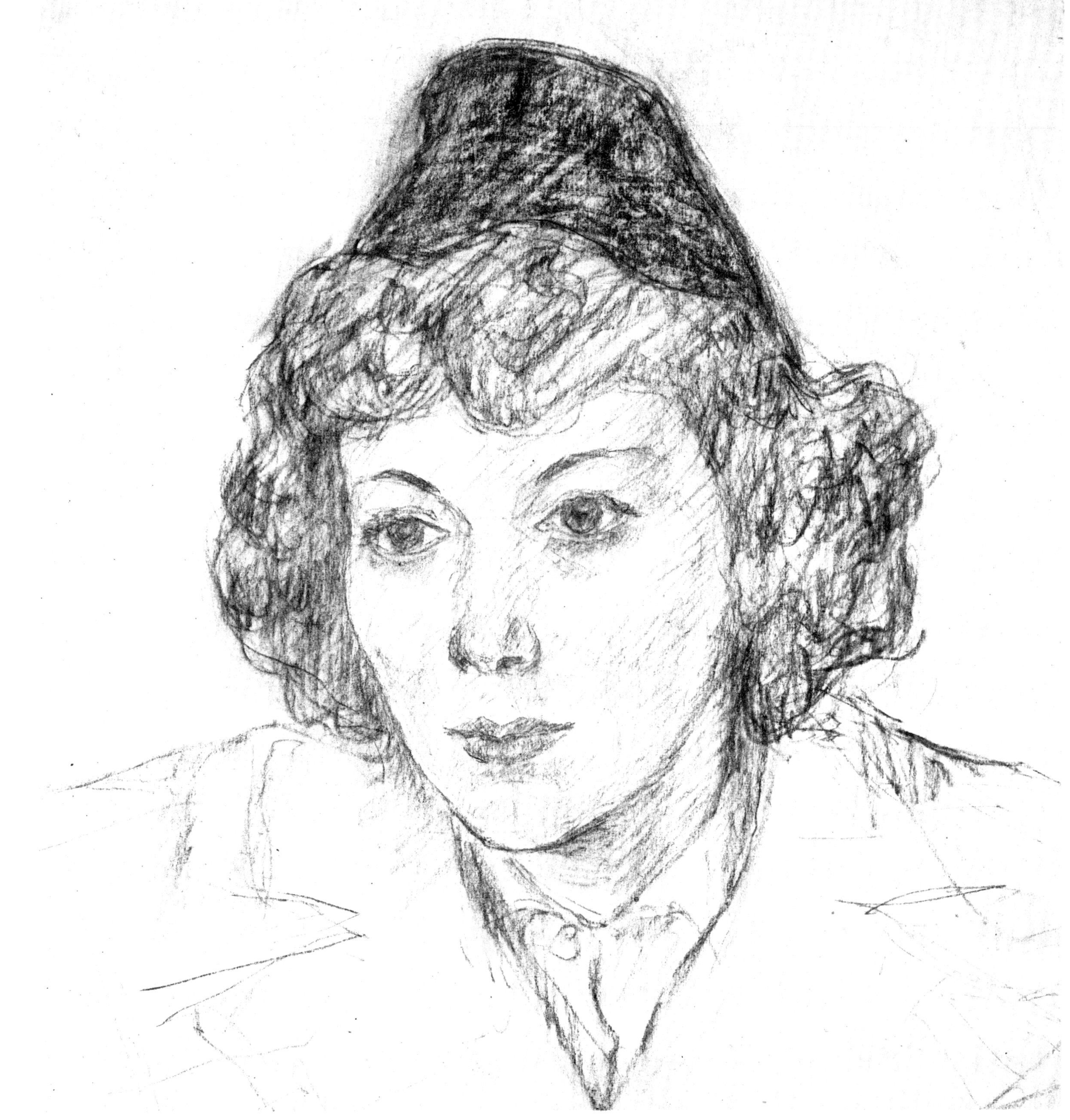

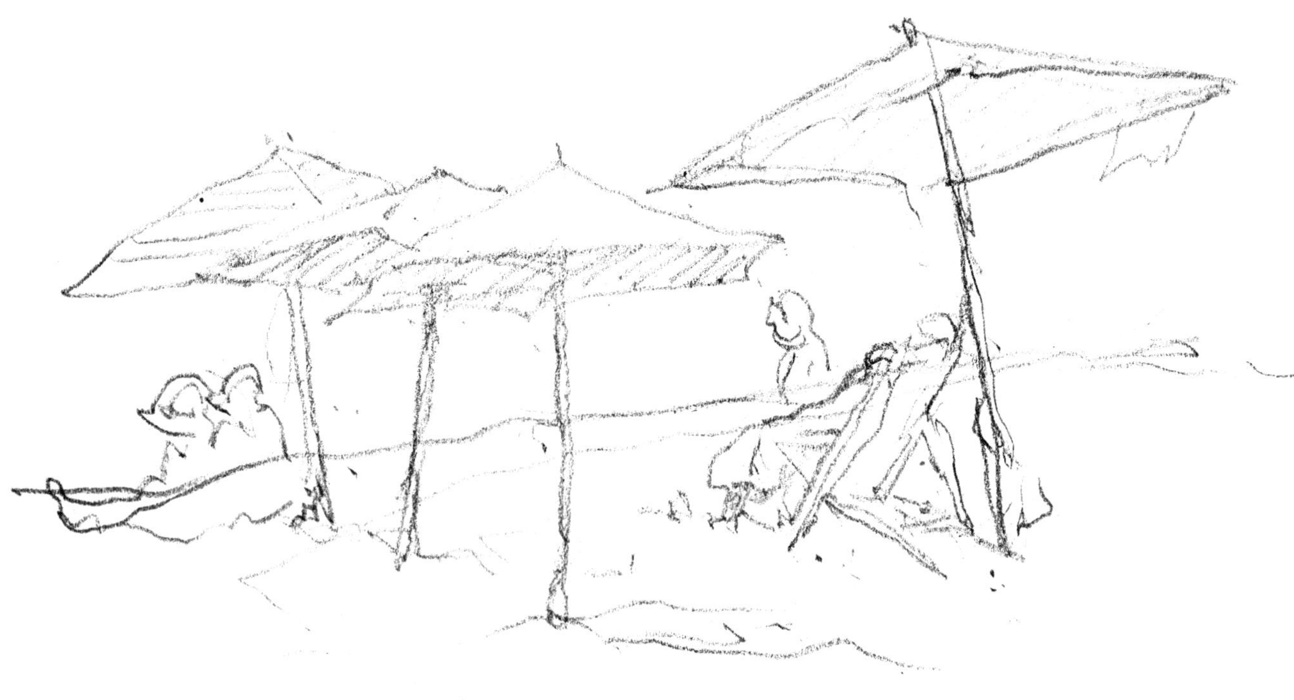

Drawing has been a constant fascination for me, and color has been increasingly fascinating. The color relations in my work have gotten more conscious as I've gotten older. I became more aware of the effects of colors and the importance of a little dissonance. Like the yellow that Bonnard uses. It can't steal the show, but it helps enormously. I've taken care to paint with clarity, not to let the color get dirty. And I've worked on developing expressive brushwork. Still, I painted just naturally.

What makes the great paintings great? First of all, the artist loves the subject and understands it thoroughly, and then renders it with all the knowledge and feeling and character that he or she has. I had a rather cynical uncle who used to say that all the great things had been done, but I don't agree with him. Each generation is different and has to try to do great things. I've always liked to think independently.

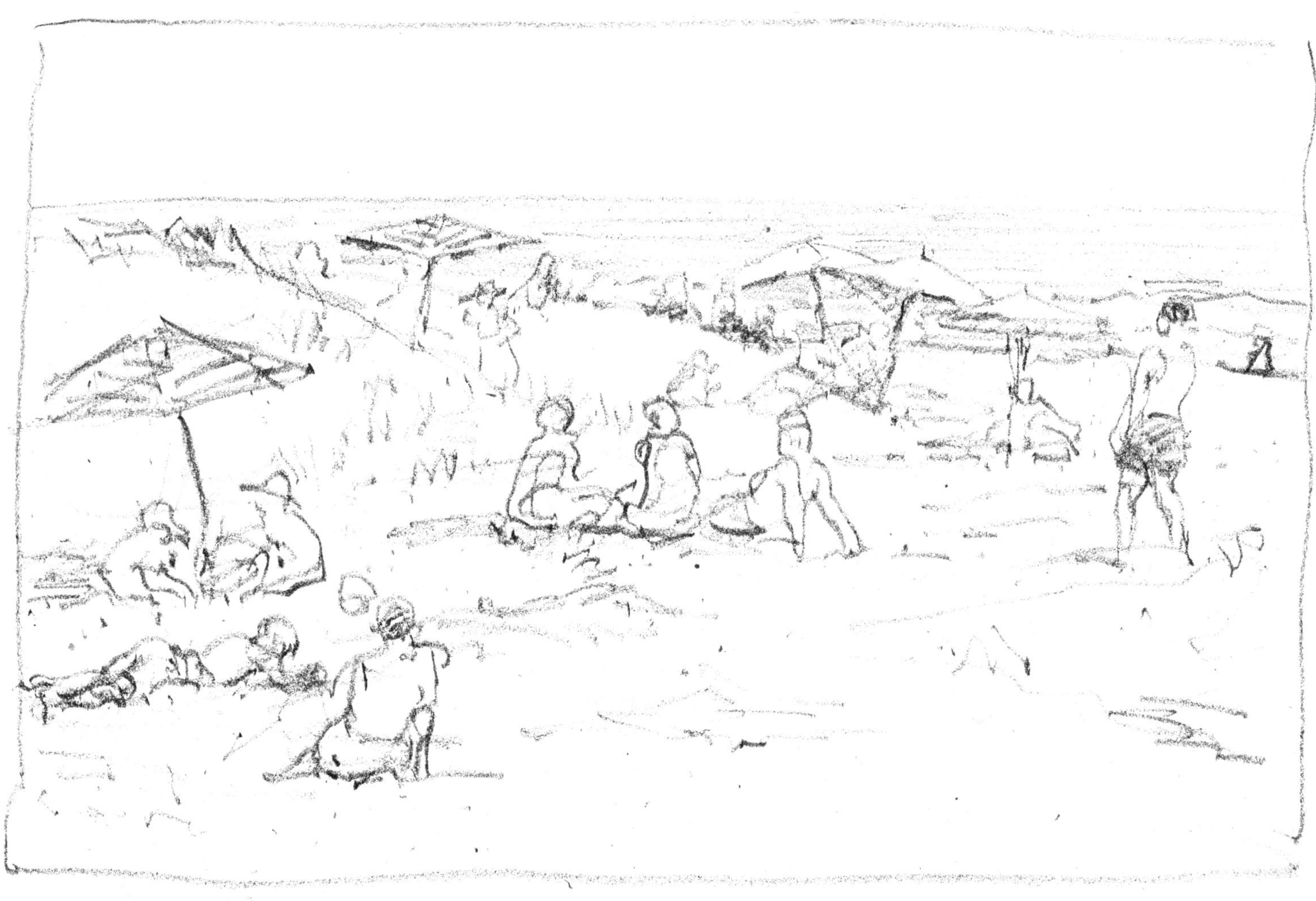

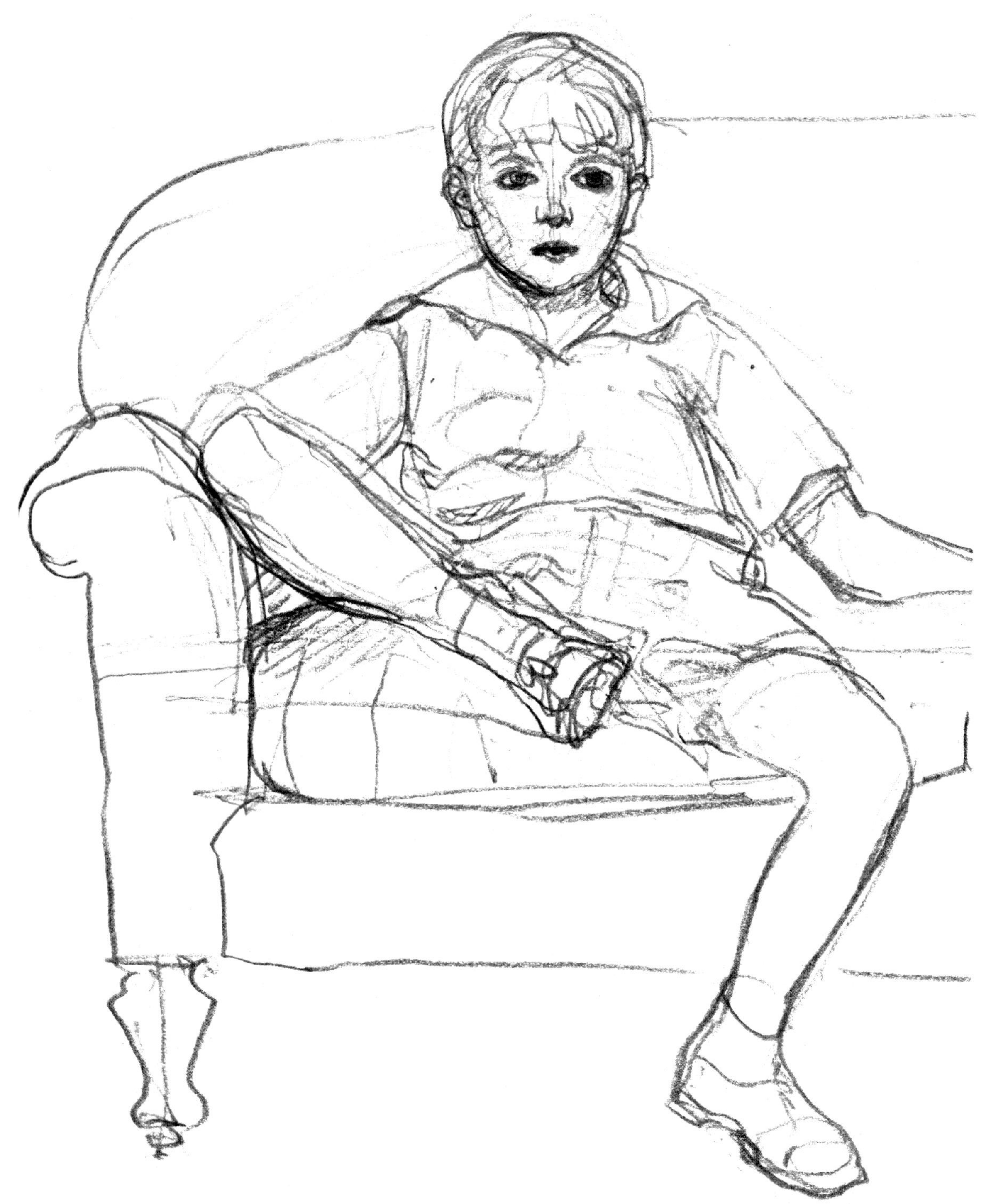

I've always tried to keep the whole in mind, the whole picture. If you lose track of the whole feeling, the whole design, you're lost. The pattern and design have to feel true.

¶

Style—that's a wonderful word, an elusive word. An artist might have style for one person and maybe not for another. Certainly painters like Bonnard and Braque had it tremendously. Picasso didn't have it in everything. Some of the paintings are too agitated and self-conscious, although they always had life.

I had the need to keep painting because I had decided to be an artist. And I was always trying to improve. I hoped to be a fine, distinguished painter, and I worked at it without the thought of wanting to startle or shock in order to make a hit. Most of my work was on my own, through observation and reading.

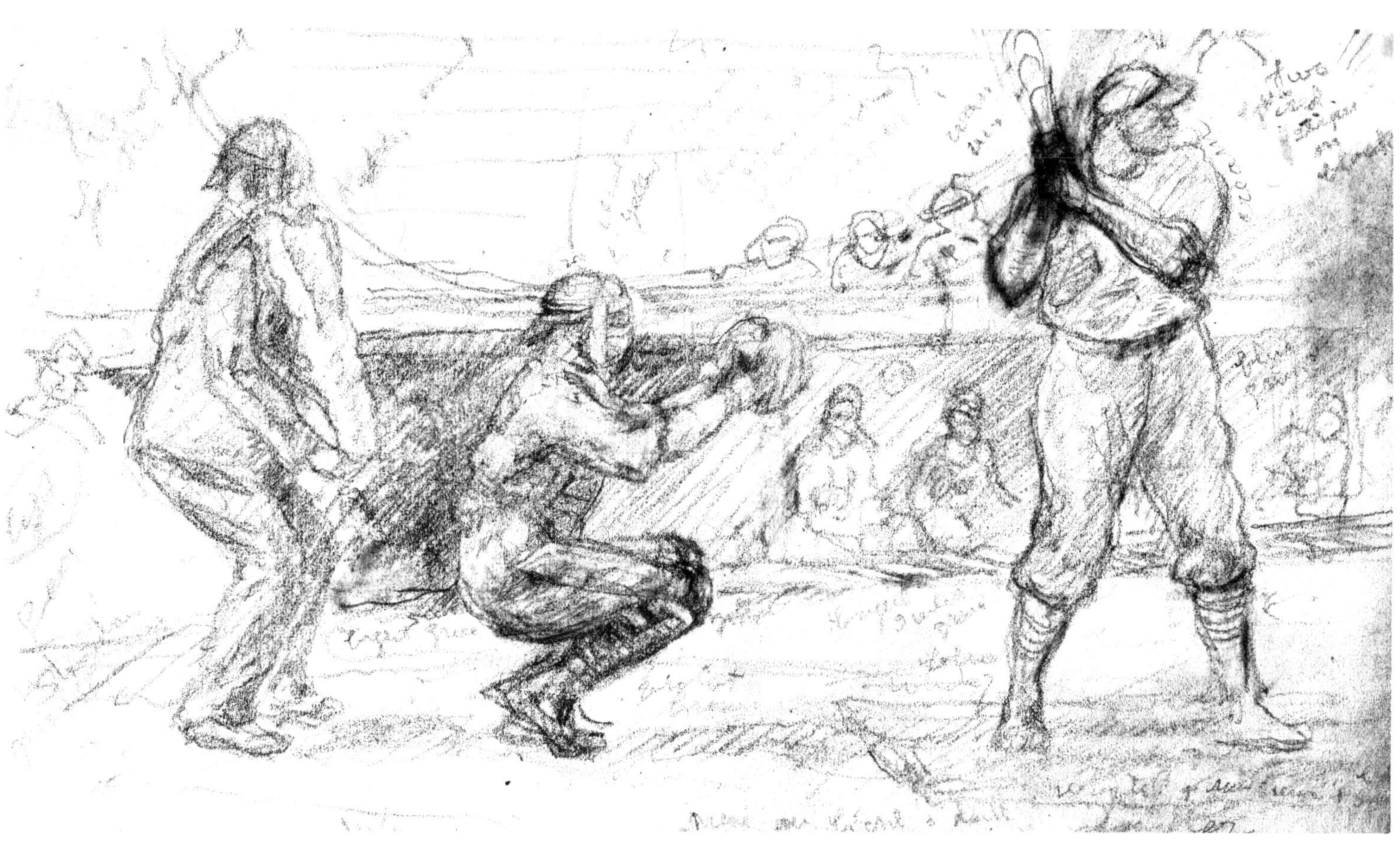

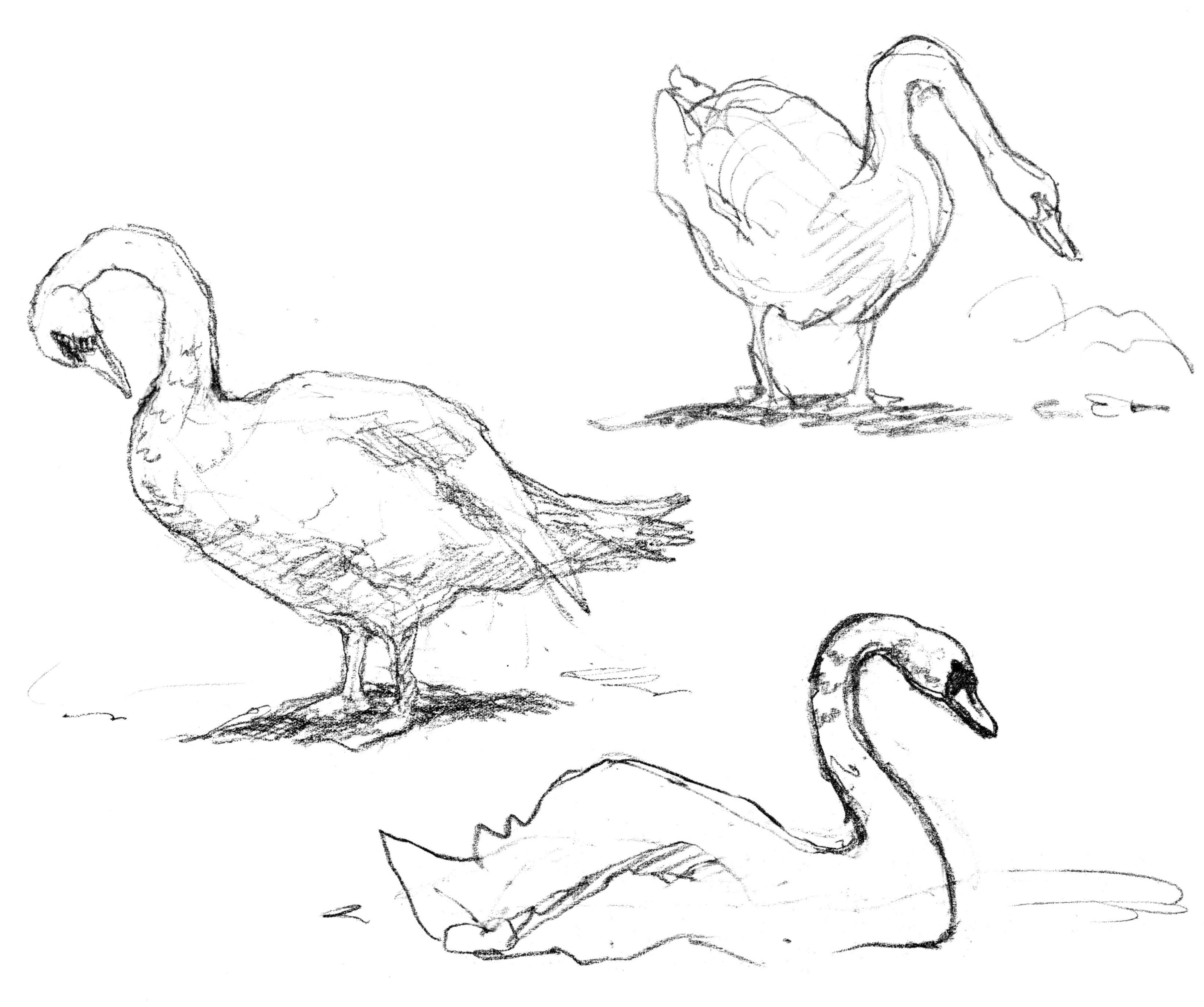

The Michelangelo David! We saw it with Charles Seymour, standing on the floor on a level with ourselves—not up on a pedestal! You could get close to it and run your hands over it or near it as Kokoschka did with all paintings, and *how* he made them come to life as he did it! Everything that was essentially art came out! If it was there he would discover it and, in a gesture over the dross-part, dismiss it!

¶

"What the heart knows today, the head will know tomorrow." That is almost the whole thing in the *making* of a work of art. For the impetus given by the love of the thing, seen or imagined, will carry through the study of the *facts*, and the designing of them and the enthusiasm and sense of the gift and wonder of the thing. Its significance in relation to the world will still be there at *the finish*.

¶

The real artists are those who have the vital spark, who don't just *make pictures*. That is *deadly*. There must be an offshoot from life in a *real picture*. It must have vitality.

¶

I think that the *means* used function just as importantly as *ends*. Their effects result in reverberations that continue.

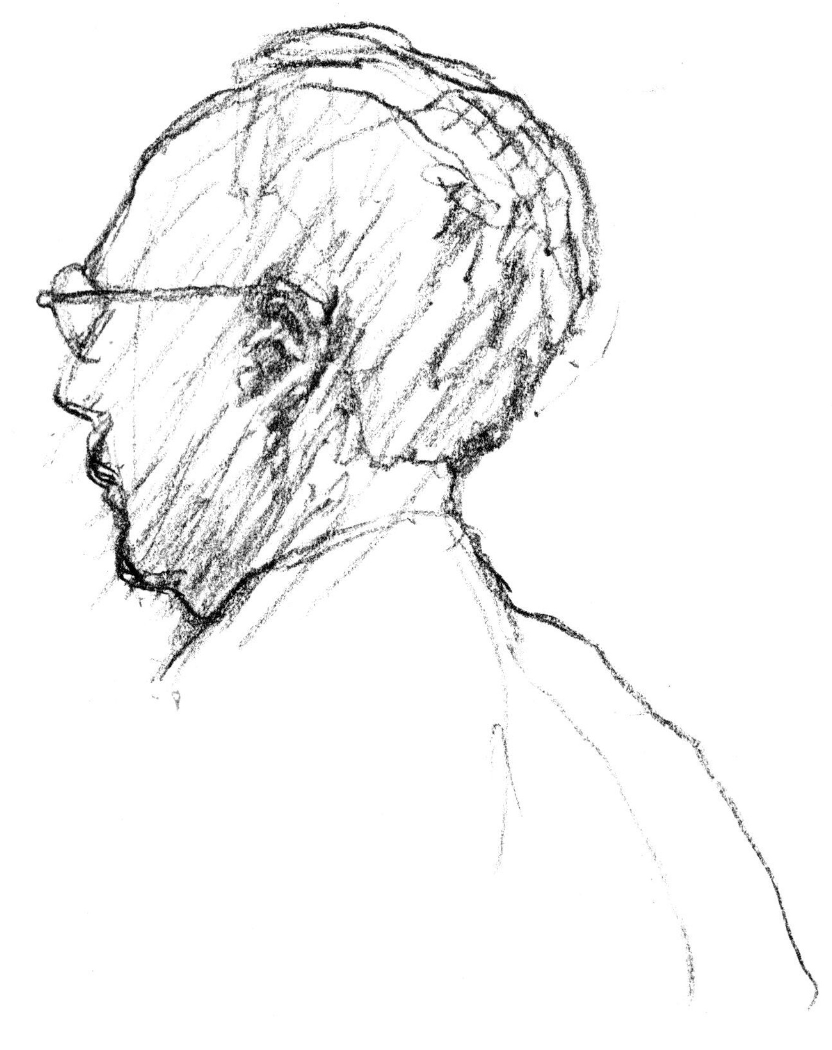

Jan 10th '60

. . . most important—more than all the pattern, design, solid form and everything else—is the spirit, the vitality, the life. With that a painting is an offshoot of life, it is sufficient in itself. Some paintings look as if they were vital sparks shot off a revolving sun and some look like great meteors off a living earth. They can display the life spark in many different ways—but it must be there.

In looking at pictures I always say to myself, Does it make me want it *and* has it life?

¶

We can't make great paintings until they are the outlet for our souls.

¶

Try to keep everything in your life in relation to the main purpose. As all relations of lines are in relation to each other and with a whole in mind, the same is so of masses, forms, shapes, and colours. "When relations are considered, form and lines are automatically controlled to that end." So in life.

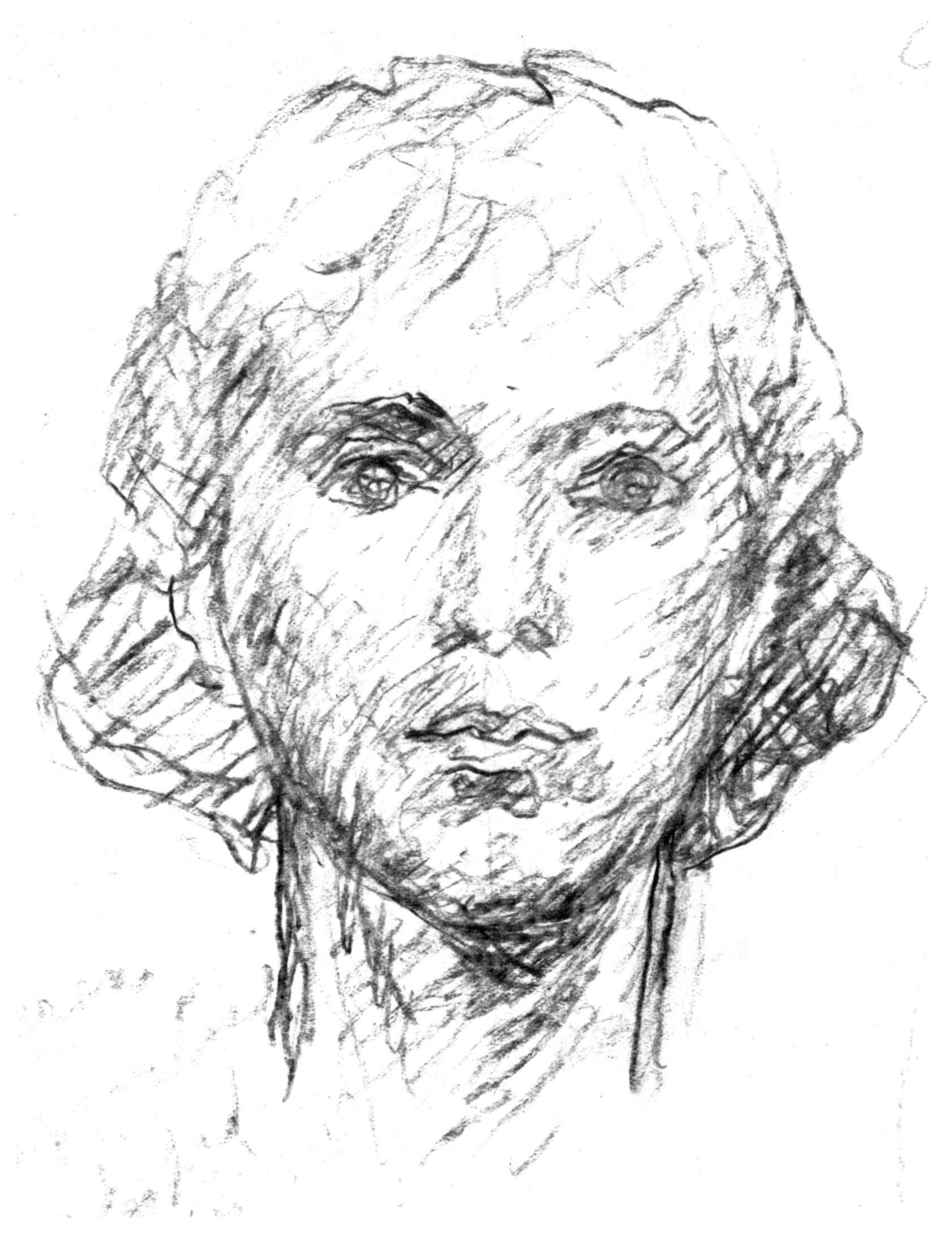

It seems that to extract the very *essence* of things, leaving out all extraneous matter and keeping the content of a picture as pure, simplified, intense and as ecstatic as possible is the excuse and real reason for a picture. One must search *within* one for that dominant, intensified personal quality that must shine out from the picture. Don't put any meaningless forms into a picture *because* they are realistic or because they would make it more recognizable. Everything must contribute to the beauty and interest of the design as a whole, the manipulation of color areas of directions and rhythms. Just as the forms are intensified and simplified (if *necessary*) so the color in every stroke must reach an apex of beauty that will be fine in itself *aside* from that which it portrays.

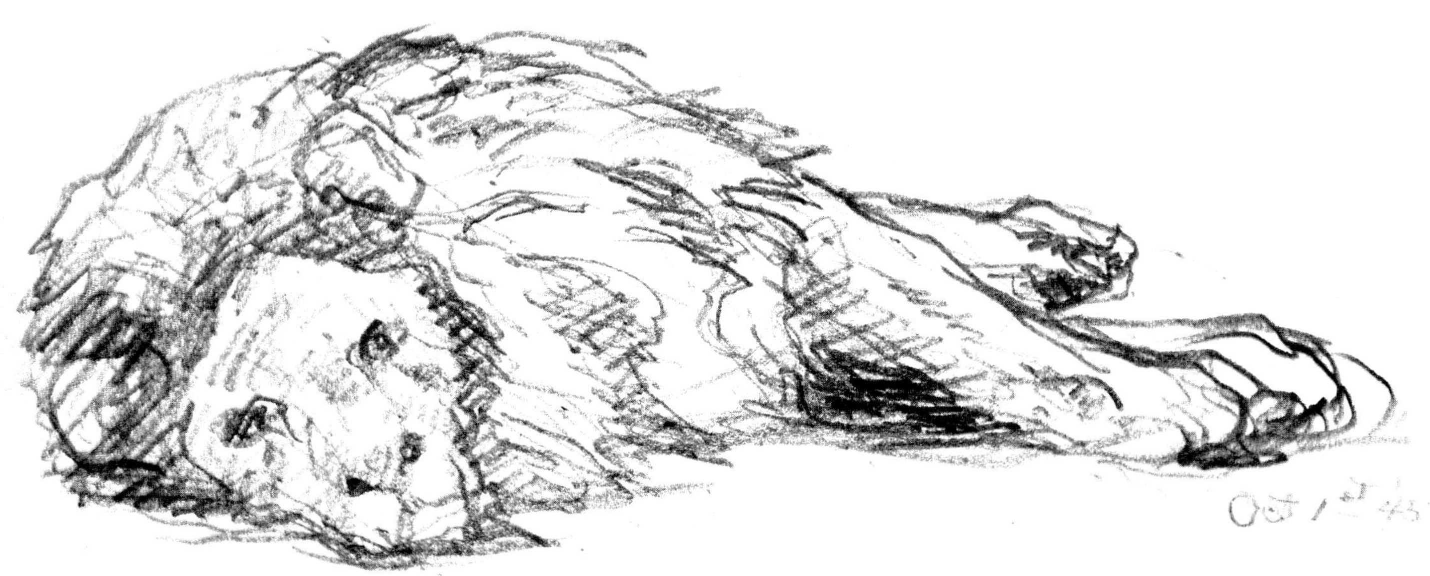

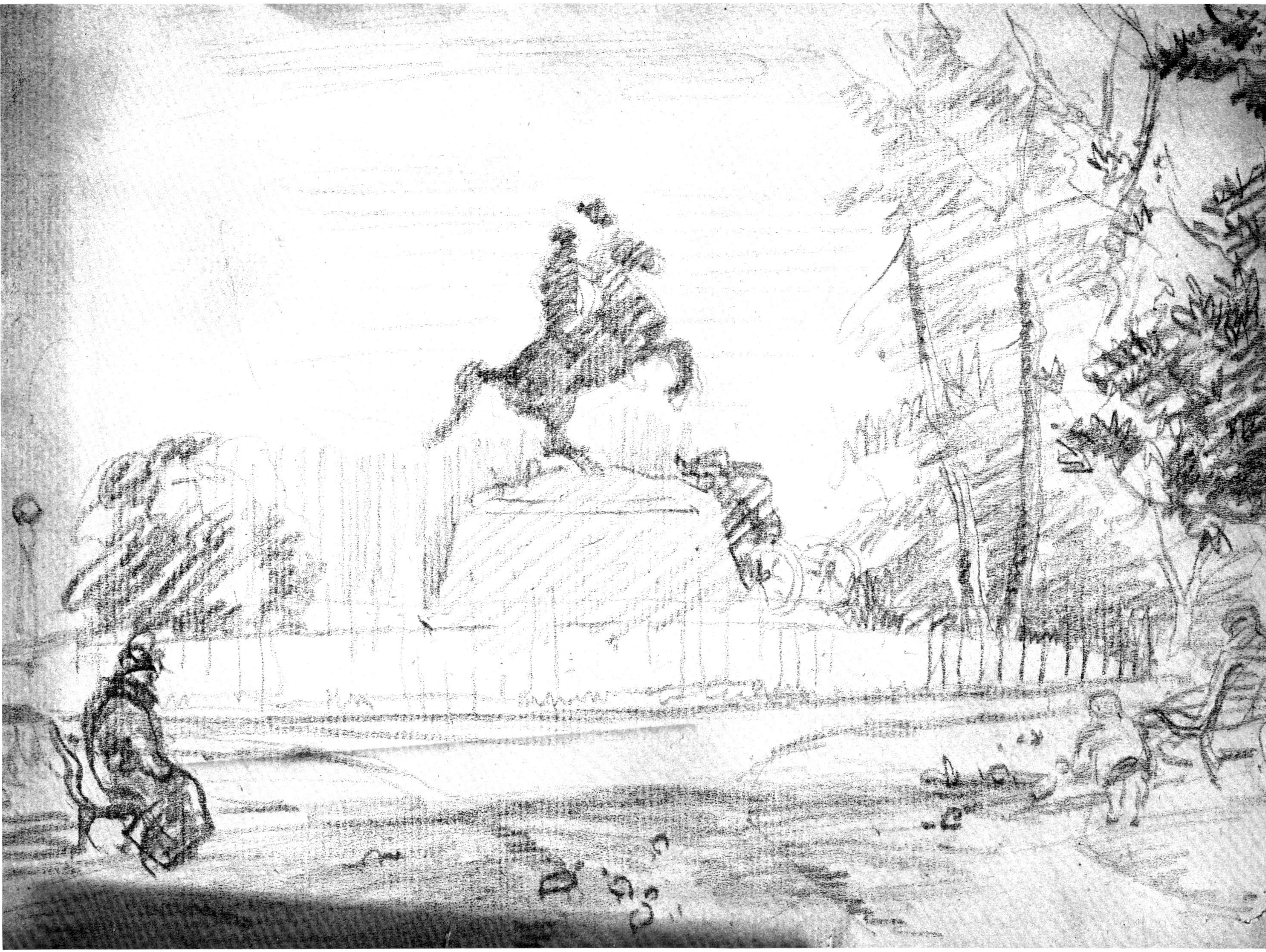

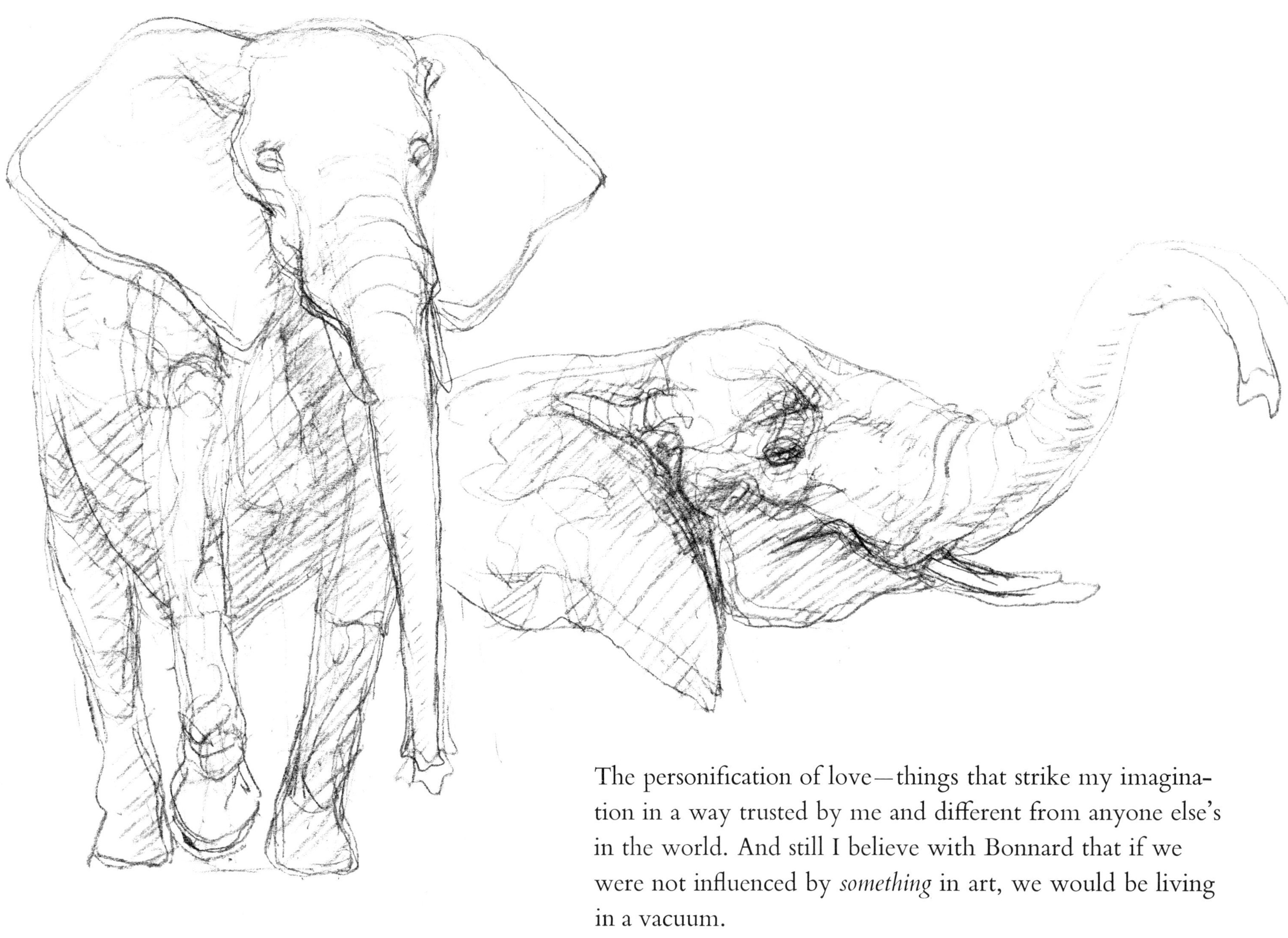

The personification of love—things that strike my imagination in a way trusted by me and different from anyone else's in the world. And still I believe with Bonnard that if we were not influenced by *something* in art, we would be living in a vacuum.

I love painting. I love the nature I paint. It means an infinite capacity for taking pains without rushing in to finish for the effect, forgetting that it needs to be alive, palpitating, each form with its multiple planes correctly placed in space and eye travel between these forms.

¶

The last strokes of a painting must be done with the same bold enthusiasm with which the first zestful strokes were done in the first flush of enthusiasm. Every stroke to the end must have the vision that made me want to do it, "the little sensation" that initiated the work. We are gods in art and the whole is felt and seen continuously *with* love, classic and joyous; space; and, if possible, humour.

¶

You can't isolate one quality and admire it. You may love blue but if you had the whole world blue you would hate it. There must be other colours, other qualities. What are they used *with*, what's their goal? Dissatisfaction with roast beef or government or life in general—is it destructive? You have to be dissatisfied in order to improve.

¶

In painting, let there be *surprise*, mystery, indefiniteness.

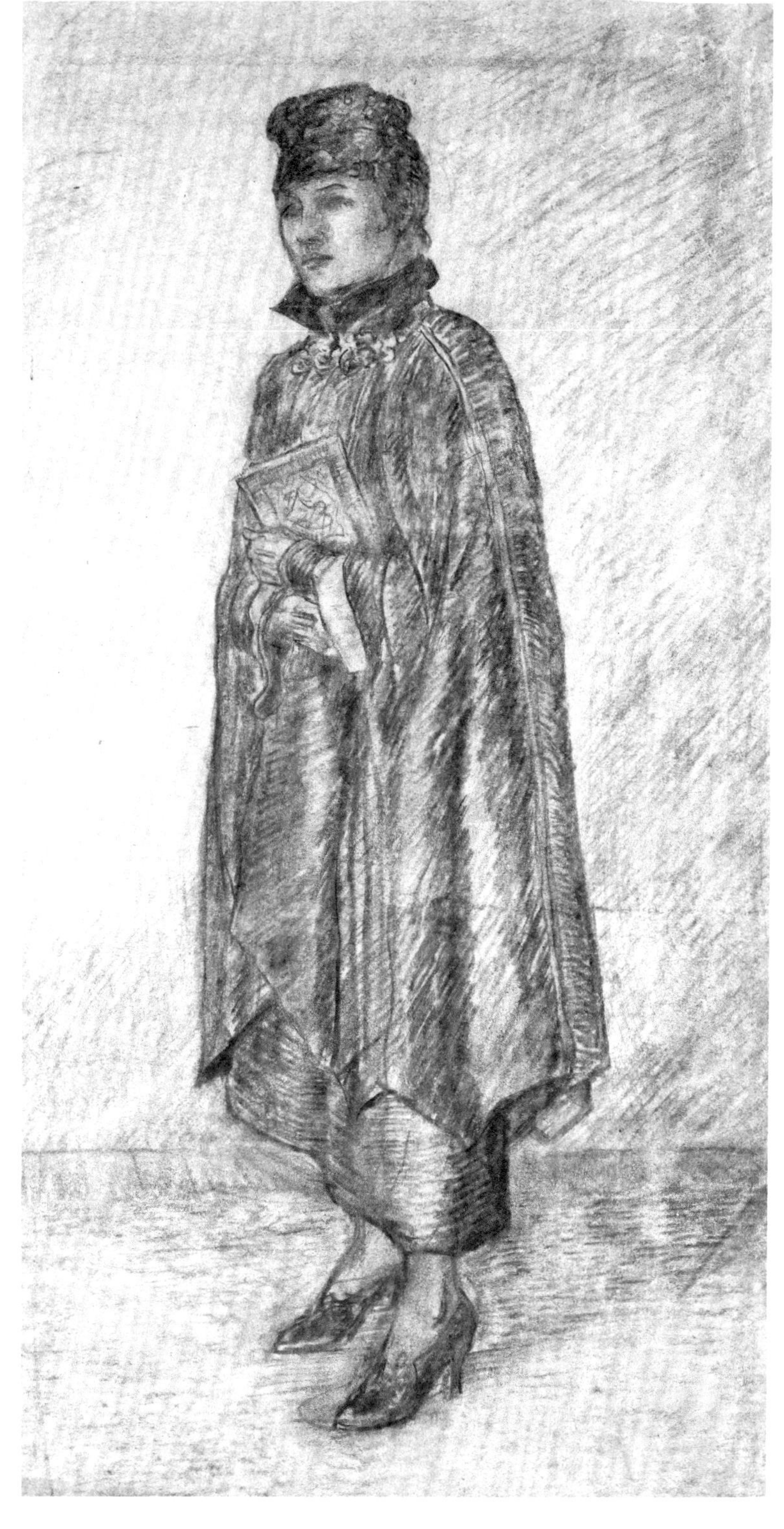

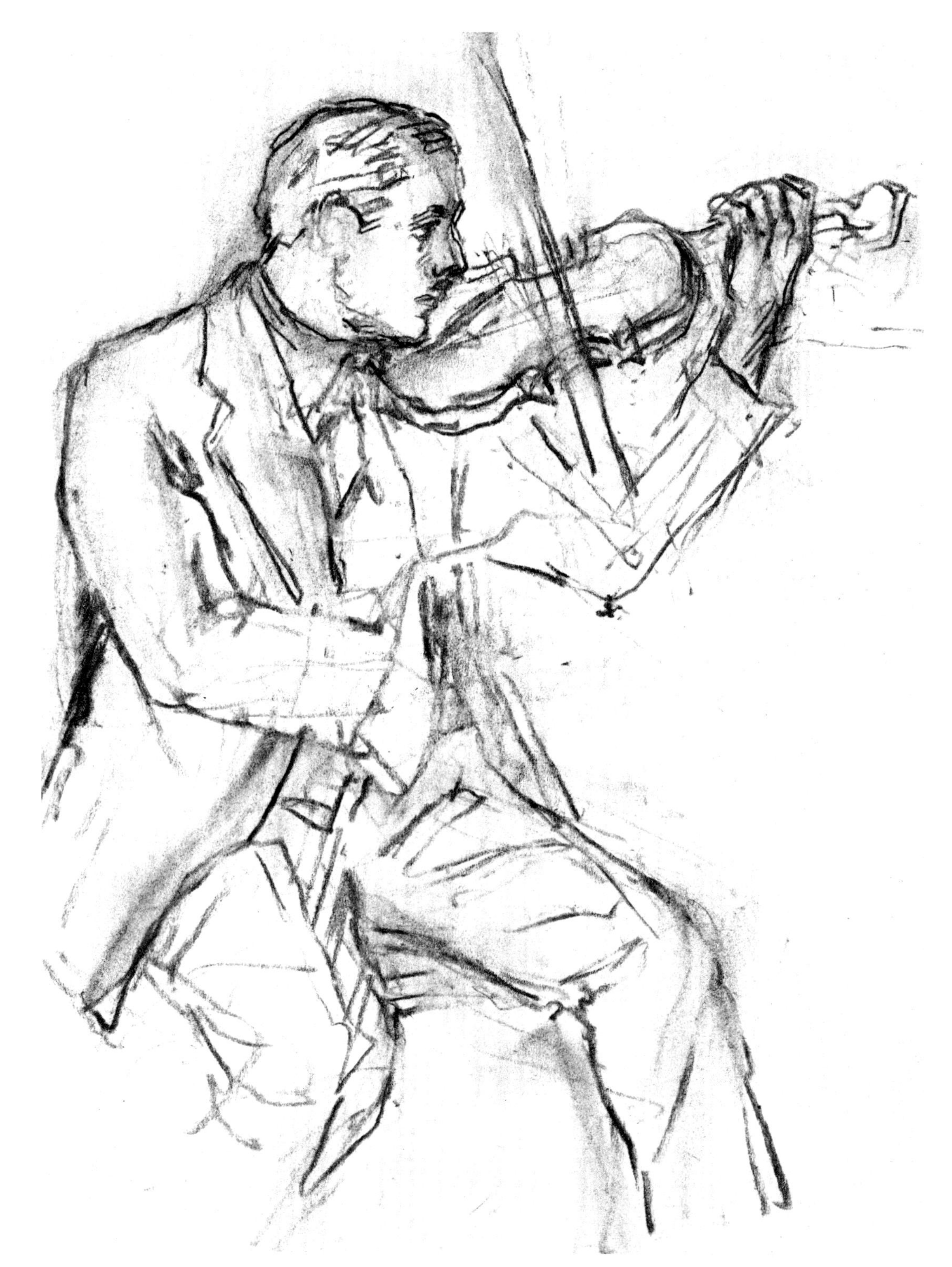

EXHIBITION HISTORY AND INDEX

One-woman Exhibitions

1923	Arts Club, Washington, D.C.
1924	C.W. Kraushaar Art Galleries, New York
1925–84	Numerous one-woman exhibitions at The Phillips Collection, Washington, D.C.
1926	Durand-Ruel Galleries, New York
1928	C.W. Kraushaar Art Galleries, New York
1929	O'Brien Galleries, Chicago
1930	C.W. Kraushaar Art Galleries, New York
1930	The Charcoal Club, Baltimore
1934	Public Library, Washington, D.C.
1941, 48	Bignou Gallery, New York
1945–46	The Santa Barbara Museum of Art, Calif.
1952, 56, 59	Durlacher Brothers, New York
1955	The Corcoran Gallery of Art, Washington, D.C.
1959	California Palace of the Legion of Honor, San Francisco
1965	The Edward W. Root Art Center, Hamilton College, Clinton, N.Y.
1973	Marlborough Fine Art Limited, London
1977	Franz Bader Gallery, Washington, D.C.
1978	Cosmos Club, Washington, D.C.
1982	The Fine Arts Center, Cheekwood, Nashville, Tenn.

Major Group Exhibitions

1921–26, 30–33, 37, 41, 44, 53, 55	The Corcoran Gallery of Art, Washington, D.C.
1922–85	Represented in numerous group exhibition and hangings of the permanent collection at The Phillips Collection, Washington, D.C.
1925, 32–33, 44, 45, 54	The Pennsylvania Academy of Fine Arts, Philadelphia, Pa.
1925–33, 35	The Cleveland Museum of Art, Ohio
1928, 29, 31–36, 40–41	The Art Institute of Chicago
1928	Anderson Galleries, New York
1929	Art Museum, Portland, Ore.
1929–32, 35–40	American Federation of Arts, New York
1930	The Museum of Modern Art, New York
1930, 31	Women's University Club, New York
1930, 31, 33, 34, 36–38, 40, 43, 44, 46–50	Museum of Fine Arts, Carnegie Institute, Pittsburgh, Pa.
1930, 33	Gallery of the Fine Arts, Yale University, New Haven, Conn.
1931	The Downtown Gallery, New York
1931–32	The Brooklyn Museum, New York
1932	Stendahl Art Gallery, Los Angeles
1932, 33, 37	Junior League, Washington, D.C.
1932–35, 53	Whitney Museum of American Art, New York

1933	Addison Gallery of American Art, Phillips Academy, Andover, Mass.
1933	Renaissance Society, Chicago
1934, 36	Rockefeller Center, New York
1934	Baltimore Museum of Art, Md.
1934	The Toledo Museum of Art, Ohio
1938, 40	Howard University, Washington, D.C.
1938	Musée de Jeu de Paume, Paris
1939	Whyte Gallery, Washington, D.C.
1939	"Golden Gate International Exposition: Contemporary Art," San Francisco
1939	Syracuse Museum, N.Y.
1939	The Century Club, N.Y.
1940	Palace of Fine Arts, San Francisco
1941	Santa Barbara Museum of Art, Calif.
1941	Wilmington Museum of Art, Del.
1945	The Art Gallery of Toronto, Canada
1946	The Tate Gallery, London
1948	The American University, Washington, D.C.
1951	The George Washington University Library, Washington, D.C.
1957, 64	Franz Bader Gallery, Washington, D.C.
1969, 79	University of Maryland Art Gallery, College Park, Md.
1972	Salem Fine Arts Center, Winston-Salem, N.C.
1972	North Carolina Museum of Art, Raleigh, N.C.
1973	The Mobile Art Gallery, Ala.
1978	Terry Dintenfass Gallery, New York
1981–83	California Palace of the Legion of Honor, San Francisco, and tour
1983	The Albany Museum of Art, Ga.

INDEX

Numerals in italics indicate an illustration of the subject cited.

A

Acker, Alice (sister), 4, 8, *12*, 17
Acker, Alice Beal (mother), *2*, 3, 4, 7, 10, 13
Acker, Charles Ernest (father), *2*, 3, 4, 10
Acker, Eleanor (sister), 4, 8, 9, *12*, 13, 28, 44
Acker, Ernest (brother), 4, *12*
Acker, Fitzgerald (nephew), 123
Acker, Marjorie Grant. *See* Phillips, Marjorie
Acker, Mary Elizabeth (sister, *now* Mrs. John Lyman), 4, 7, 8, 10, 11, *12*
Acker, Mercia Grant (paternal grandmother), 3
Acker, William (brother), 4, 8, *12*, 28, 40
Acker, William James (paternal grandfather), 3

B

Basket of Grapes, 54, *55*
Basket of Peaches, 58, *59*
Beal, Eleanor Louise (maternal grandmother), 4, 5, 28, 46
Beal, Gifford (uncle), 5, 7, 13–14
Beal, Mary (aunt), 28, 46
Beal, Maude (aunt, Mrs. Gifford Beal), 13, 14
Beal, Reynolds (uncle), 5, 7
Beal, William Reynolds (maternal grandfather), 3, 4, 5, 28
Before Supper, 34, *35*
Bell, Clive, 38
Big Barn on a Hill, 60, *61*
Big Pear, The, 76, *77*
Bolduan, Ruth, 23, 24
Bonnard, Pierre, 22, 28, 51, 96, 103, 106, 108, 116; *The Old Horse*, 22; *The Open Window*, 22
Braque, Georges, 108
Breakfast Room, 36, *37*
Brown, Louis, 28
Buzzard, The, 22, 64, *65*

C

Calder, Alexander, 21, 26
Calder, Peggy, 26
California Palace of the Legion of Honor, 82
Carlisle, Leila, 30
Carlisle, Lister, 30
Cézanne, Paul, ix, 21
Chase, William Merritt, 7
Clarke, Bert, v
Cocoanut Grove, 44, *45*
Conversation Piece, 72, *73*, 92

D

DiMaggio, Joe, 68
Dove, Arthur, 64
Dreier, Katherine, 13, 64
Duchamp, Marcel, 64
Duncan Phillips and His Collection (book), ix, 21
Dunmarlin, 19

E

Earliest Tulips, 90, *91*
Edge of Aunt Mary's Garden, An (Marjorie Acker), 28, *29*

F

Family at Dinner (Marjorie Acker), 10, *11*

G

Gasper, Barbara, v
Gerson, Miss Virginia, 7
Gilliam, Sam, 21

Giotto, 104
Gray, Cleve, 21
Griswold, Mrs., 21–22
Grove, Bob, v

H

Hare, David, 21
Hope, Mr. and Mrs. Anthony, 38
Hosefros, Paul, 20
Hudson at Ossining, The (Marjorie Acker), 26, *27*
Huxley, Judith, 90
Huxley, Matthew, 90

K

Kipling, R., 3
Kokoschka, O., 111

L

Laughlin and Baby Duncan, 88, *89*
Lindbergh, Charles, 56
Little Bouquet, 46, *47*, 62
Lippman, Walter, 92
Locust Trees in Spring, 48, *49*, *50*
Lyman, Mrs. John. *See* Acker, Mary Elizabeth

M

McLaughlin, Jim, 58
Marshall Neil Roses (Marjorie Acker), 14, *15*
Maypole, 42, *43*
Mehring, Howard, 21
Michelangelo, 111
Miller, Kenneth Hayes, 13
Mitchell, Henry, 94
Mitchell, Virginia, 94
Mixed Bouquet, 94, *95*
Monet, Claude, 103
Morning Walk, 56, *57*, 72

N

Nasturtiums, 70, *71*
Nectarines and Bottle of Wine, 84, *85*
Night Baseball, 68, *69*
North Library, 16–17, *17*
Nuns on the Roof, 30, *31*

O

Open Door, The, 78, *79*
Orchid and Palette, 67, *68*

P

Parsons, Betty, 84
Partridge, Sylvia (niece), v, x, 23, 80, 101
Path to the Studio, 80, *81*
Penalba, Alicia, 21
Pep II, v, 23
Phillips, Betty (former daughter-in-law), 88
Phillips, Duncan (husband), 14, 28, 32, 44, 54, 62
    death, ix, 18, 20, 21, 92
    in MP's paintings, *37*, 72, *73*, 92, *93*
    as painter, 58, 60
    and The Phillips Collection, 14, 21, 70, 103
    photographs of, *18*, *19*
Phillips, Major Duncan Clinch (father-in-law), 17
Phillips, Duncan Vance (grandson), *24*, 60, 88, *89*
Phillips, Gifford (cousin), 58
Phillips, Jennifer (daughter-in-law), 40
Phillips, Laughlin (son), v, ix–x, 16, 18, *19*, 21, 23, *24*, 34, 36, 56, 58, 62, 72, 88, *89*, 92
Phillips, Liza (granddaughter), 23, *24*, 54, 72
Phillips, Mary Marjorie (daughter), 16, 32, 36, 40
Phillips, Marjorie (*née* Acker)
    birth, 3–4
    childhood, 4, 7
    drawings by, *50*, *102*, *105*, *106*, *107*, *108*, *109*, *110*, *112*, *113*, *114*, *115*, *116*, *117*, *118*
    education and teachers, 5, 10, 13

exhibitions, 119–20
and her husband and family, 7, 14, 16, 18, 19, 20–21, 26, 28, 30, 36, 40, 46, 54, 62, 68, 72, 88, 92
ideas about art, ix–x, 38, 40, 42, 48, 51, 56, 58, 60, 74, 76, 78, 80, 96, 103–18
importance of art to, 4, 5, 19, 23, 44
influences on her art, 4, 5, 7, 10, 13–14, 16, 22, 26, 38, 96
and "The Magazine," 7–9
other interests and responsibilities, ix, 9, 18, 20–21
photographs of, *ii*, *12*, *18*, *19*, *23*, *24*
self-portraits and in her paintings, *9*, *17*, 28, *29*, 36, *37*, 56, *57*, 72, *73*, 96, *97*
See also titles of works
Phillips, Mother (mother-in-law), 14, 16, 17, 19, 36, 46, 72
Phillips Collection, The, ix, x, 14, *16*, 16n, 17, 18, 21, 22, 23, 26, 30, 32, 36, 42, 46, 48, 51, 56, 58, 64, 66, 68, 70, 74, 76, 78, 86, 92, 96, 98, 103
Philodendron, 74, *75*
Picasso, Pablo, 21, 108
Piero della Francesca, 80, 104
Poppies, 38, *39*
Portrait of Duncan, 92, *93*
Pratt, Mr., 22
Purves, Carroll (Mrs. Edmund R. Purves), 22

R

Renoir, A., *Luncheon of the Boating Party*, *24*, 32
Robinson, Boardman, 13
Roses in a Lalique Bowl, 98, *99*
Roses, Marshall Neil, 14
Rothko, Mark, *Green and Maroon*, 21
Rue de la Boetie, 32, 33

S

Self Portrait, 96, *97*
Seymour, Charles, 111
Simuro, John (chauffeur), 34, 60
Siprell, Clara, 18
Smith college, 82
Snead, Bill, 23
Société Anonyme, 13, 64
Still, Clyfford, 21
Summer Morning, 34, 40, *41*

T

Tack, Augustus Vincent, 17
Terrasse, Mr., 22
Torch Flowers Against Coral, 82, *83*
Town and Mountains, 86, *87*

U

Untitled works (Marjorie Acker), *6*, 7, *8*, *9*

V

Violets and Gardenia, 62, *63*

W

Watteau, 103, 104
Wilellyn, 28
Woods and Farms, 51, *52–53*

Y

Youngerman, Jack, 21

Composed in English Monotype Bembo and
printed by offset lithography on Warren's Lustro Dull
by A. Colish, Inc., Mount Vernon, New York.
Binding by Publishers Book Bindery,
Long Island City, New York.
Designed by Bert Clarke.